A FIGHT AGAINST THE ODDS

A FIGHT AGAINST THE ODDS

LIFE GROWING UP IN JERSEY CITY AND PLAYING BASKETBALL FOR THE LEGENDARY COACH BOB HURLEY

Shelton T. Gibbs

ISBN: 0999311824
ISBN 13: 9780999311820
Library of Congress Control Number: 2017953477
AFATO, Union, NJ

To my parents,
Shelton and Elyse Gibbs
Thank you for all that you have done and continue to do for Shellyse, Shyquan, and me. Your love, dedication, and sacrifices are sincerely appreciated.

In Jersey City, it seemed like there was always one thing guaranteed to find you: trouble. Even when you tried your best to stay away from it, somehow trouble always found its way to you. This is an inspiring story about seven kids from the streets of Jersey City that were inseparable. Seven kids who stuck together no matter what came their way. The love for basketball brought them all together, giving them a reason to fight for more. Ultimately, they all followed different paths, but the bond they developed seemed to be everlasting.

In *A Fight Against The Odds*, Shelton T. Gibbs will cover the struggles the seven had coming from the jagged areas of Jersey City and playing basketball for a very high demanding coach, Bob Hurley. In the streets, there were drugs, alcohol, prostitution, fighting, and gun violence. Yet, in Coach Hurley's gym, there was a basketball court, Coach Hurley, and his high demanding expectations for perfection. With no room for the streets to carry over into Coach Hurley's gym, the crew had to juggle between following the right path or being sucked into the negativity that surrounded them. Basketball made the decision easier for some, while others couldn't handle the adversity of dealing with the hardship from the streets and those very high demands from the Legendary Coach Bob Hurley.

CONTENTS

Cover Design: ilovemycover.com
Cover Photo: Omar Zamrudeen
Back Cover Photos: St. Anthony Year Books 2001-2003

Photo on page 210 by Niiya Ruth

All other photos provided by Author and from St. Anthony High School Year Books 2001-2004

This is a work of Non-fiction. All things talked about in this book were personally experienced by Author.

Please visit www.afightagainsttheodds.com with any feedback.

A LETTER TO SISTER ALAN

Dear Sister Alan,

There are not enough words that can express how grateful I am to have had you in my life. You were always so kind and nurturing, like a second mother. It just came so naturally to you. When any of us were feeling down and unsure about ourselves, you knew just what to say to uplift our spirits. You kept us in line and made sure we did what we needed to do. There were times we got under your skin and angered you. There were times we made you smile and laugh. Through everything, you showed that you cared and that you loved us. We loved you as well. I was saddened to hear about your condition, but I was so proud of the fight that you had in you. You never let it show. Through everything, you never let it show. You continued to give it your all. That, Sister Alan, was true courage. A true selfless act. The way you cared and put others before yourself knowing that you were sick. I can't pretend to imagine how hard that must have been for you. You knew how difficult it was for us playing for Coach Hurley and the pressure we sometimes felt. Just your words of encouragement and your gentle hug, ending with a pat on the back was enough to brighten up the day. I must say, back then I appreciated it and now I appreciate it even more.

I wish I could hug you one last time and be granted the opportunity to hear your voice. I love you, Sister Alan. May you rest well.

Love, Shelton

Sister Mary Alan posing with Championship Trophy. 2002

I AM MY BROTHER'S KEEPER

THERE COMES A time in your life when you have to step back, take a second to think about your mistakes and what kind of character you portray yourself to be. When you have to try to adjust your behavior and put your focus towards being positive even with all the negativity around you; when you have to listen instead of always being heard. Maybe even learn to follow the positive crowd, in order to one day become a positive leader and role model yourself.

With that said, I must say that our interesting group could care less about any of that while we were coming up as kids. We could care less about how people viewed us or what they thought about us, because in our eyes we were our brother's keepers. No one would ever have our backs like we had each other's backs. No one!

You may have read about our story through a great sports writer by the name of Adrian Wojnarowski, in his book titled *The Miracle Of St. Anthony*. Or maybe you have read *Chasing Perfect,* a book written by Coach Bob Hurley with Daniel Paisner. A chapter from *Chasing Perfect* was dedicated to our 2003-2004 undefeated team. However, I have to explain this journey in my own words.

This is a story about Marcus Williams, Otis Campbell, Ahmad Mosby, Matthew Givens, Lamar Alston, Jameel George, and me, Shelton Gibbs. I will reflect on how it was playing for Coach Bob Hurley and the St. Anthony's program. The difficulties of growing up on the wild streets of Jersey City, along with the obstacles that we encountered within the streets. The reputation you had to have and much more.

Jameel (Milly) George and Marcus (M.Dot) Williams went to Public School #40 towards the Curries Woods section of Jersey City. They both lived in Curries Woods Projects at the time and played for the Public School #40 basketball team dominating their area. Marcus had arms longer than a baseball bat. We knew this because during his elementary school baseball career they took a bat and told Marcus to compare his arm span to the baseball bat. He was dunking the basketball on regulation rims in the sixth-grade. I don't know if any of the old-timers were doing that, but Marcus Williams was. He was the most athletic sixth-grader and the talk around town.

Everyone knew about Marcus Williams, and everyone knew Curries Woods Projects. Marcus and Milly were being raised in what was known as the roughest projects in Jersey City. An immigrant needed his/her green card to enjoy a free stay in the United States of America, and the average person needed a green card just to walk through Curries Woods Projects.

Marcus was raised in a single-parent home by his mother along with his older brother and younger sister, and he never really met his dad. So not only did he have the pressure as a kid dealing with not knowing his father, he had to deal with the pressure of growing up and living in Curries Woods Projects. Milly was in a similar situation. They both grew up being raised by their mothers, and I would believe it to be a hard situation, but I couldn't relate to it at all. It didn't seem to bother them, but it would sometimes slip out of their mouths once in a while. Yet, those conversations were very short lived.

As kids, who were they supposed to look up to as male figures? Who were the male adult figures in their lives that would teach them to be men? Who would be their father figures and teach them to ride their first bicycles? I'm going to give you the straightforward and raw answer. The streets would teach them everything they needed to know. Their mothers loved and nurtured them, but Curries Woods Projects were their fathers. Curries Woods Projects would teach them in the roughest and toughest way possible, how to be men.

Ahmad (Beanie) Mosby, Otis (ODB) Campbell, and me, Shelton (Lil-Ice) Gibbs went to Public School #34 in the Greenville section of Jersey City. At the time, Beanie and I lived on Warner Avenue, and Otis lived on Armstrong Avenue which was also called "The Jungle." The drug dealers, prostitutes, and gunslingers would crowd the corners of both of our blocks, but we found our way around it with basketball.

We all played basketball in the local gyms and on the playgrounds, so we were popular around our way. Ahmad and I played basketball for the Boys & Girls Club. We found out that Ahmad's dad and my mother were first cousins during our years in Public School #34. We were very excited about finding out we were family. All this time we knew each other, we didn't have the slightest idea that we were cousins. Beanie and I played for Sacred Heart Elementary School, Catholic Youth Organization (CYO) team because our school didn't have a CYO team. Matthew was another player that played for Sacred Heart but attended another school. Beanie ended up moving to Hudson Garden Projects and transferring schools, but Otis and I stayed in 34.

Like Marcus and Milly, Beanie and Otis also lived in homes without their fathers. Ahmad's dad passed away when he was young, and he also grew up in a home being raised by his mother. Beanie was the youngest of three sisters and an older brother who was living the street life. As kids, even the older kids would fear Beanie because of the reputation his brother had.

When we were in the fourth-grade, an eighth-grader took something I made for my mother and threw it in the sewer. It made me furious, so furious that as a fourth-grader I forgot this eighth-grader was about two feet taller than me and probably ten times stronger than me; that didn't stop me from punching this kid square in the face a few times to relieve my anger. As I turned and walked away, just like the coward he was, he crept up behind me and started to choke me.

Now, this is how much the older kids feared Beanie because of his brother. Beanie was in the same grade as me and a little shorter than I was. When he found out about it he was pissed. What a coincidence that the fourth-graders and eighth-graders had the same lunch periods. The next day in school, the little fourth-grader Beanie beat up this eighth-grader and he didn't even defend himself. He allowed Beanie to whip on him like he stole something and begged for him not to tell his brother.

Beanie was nowhere near being a bully, and he didn't quite follow his brother's path. Still, his brother taught him not to be a punk or let people get over on him. His brother taught him to fight and a good fighter he was. His brother taught him to always stand tall, never allow anyone in his personal space, and that he did. This was Beanie's father figure, his brother who was just a few years older than him and had the opportunity to spend a little more time with their dad than Beanie did.

Otis was being raised in a home with his mother, but his father was somewhat in the picture. His father and mother were separated, and he would see his dad from time to time. Not as much as he would like to see him, but he got the chance to spend a little time with him. Otis, his older brother, and mother, lived directly across the street from his grandparents, aunts, uncles, and cousins. This granted him the opportunity to have a strong family presence and several male figures to fill the voids of his dad. However, even with all that family presence immediately available, trouble wasn't too far.

Otis lived right next door to a basketball court. He could literally jump out of his window and be on the basketball court. Sounds like a good thing, but not much of a good thing when the drug dealers crowd the courts all day and night. Luckily Otis was respected by the drug dealers because he could fight and shoot a hell of a jump shot. So every now and then when he did roll out of his bed to jump out of his window and play basketball, he would have access to the court.

Still come night time the court was a dangerous spot to be, everyone knew about those courts. There were no street lights, leaving the courts pitch black when the sun went down. You could walk through the basketball court to get to the next block over, if you dared. It would be at your own risk because you never knew what animal, what street junky, or what barrel of a pistol you would end up staring down by walking through that court late at night. For that reason, it gained its street name "The Jungle," because at night it was like a jungle out there.

I was fortunate out of the crew, along with Matthew. When I say fortunate, it just means that we had the privilege of growing up with both parents at home. I lived in a home with my younger sister and brother, raised by my mother and father, Shelton and Elyse Gibbs. My father was a great basketball player who played for Snyder High School and St. Peters College holding several records. He worked as a Probation Officer and also coached basketball at Snyder High School when I was coming up. Around town, everyone would tell me how good of a player he was and revisit stories of an amazing dunk or two they saw him do. I loved to hear the stories, and I thrived to be the player he was and even better.

I was the complete opposite from all of my friends; I had both parents at home to constantly stay on me. I felt uncomfortable talking to them about my dad because they weren't being raised like me. I didn't want to trigger any thoughts of their fathers not being around, so I would only talk about my mother. At times, I even tried to stray away from my father just so I could see what it felt like to go without a father.

I didn't have the freedom the others had. When they were in the streets, I was in the house. When they were out partying, I was home watching television, playing video games, or doing pushups. I wanted to hang out in the streets as well; I wanted to know what it was like to party. I wanted to do all of the unimportant things, but not once did I think of how foolish those things were when my friends didn't even have their fathers at all.

So just like a kid, I would sacrifice being put on punishment just to see how it felt to stay out late or party. Just to see how it was to do the things my friends were doing. I wanted to fit in. Having both parents was something that we didn't have in common, but growing up in rough neighborhoods was something that we all definitely shared.

Matthew (Matt) Givens went to several elementary schools but would finish his years off at Public School #41. He was raised on Grant Avenue, yet another block crowded with drug dealers and pistol packers. Not too far from Lamar (Smiley/L) Austin who lived one or two blocks away on Garfield Avenue. They lived smack in the middle of two infamous families. We'll just call them the "Pocket Snatchers" and the "Smash Brothers."

The Pocket Snatchers were known as neighborhood bullies. If they saw it and wanted it, they would get it any way deemed necessary. The same style that the Smash Brothers would use, but the Smash Brothers were a little older and at the time considered to be a lot more dangerous. They were the neighborhood gangsters, and if you saw them even as elementary school kids, you knew to clear the area. They could care less of your age, and instead of going through the hassle, you would much rather figure out a way to avoid it.

Matt was raised by both of his parents along with his older sister on Grant Avenue. It wasn't easy growing up in the middle of two infamous families who lived strictly by the code of street life and had no remorse for others. Matt's parents were very caring and raised Matt to go to church and he even went to Sunday School. Yet, growing up in church and going to Sunday School once a week was no match for the street festivities Matt would endure every day. He had to encounter run-ins with the Pocket Snatchers every day. It eventually led to the old saying, "If you can't beat them, join them," and that's exactly what Matt did.

What kid wants to fight every day and go through living the life of constantly dipping and dodging a crew of kids that might try and beat up on you while you're alone? Yeah, it was easy to go to your parents and say 'Mom, Dad these kids are constantly on my case and I keep fighting and fighting.' Which would lead to a parent meeting, but the only thing was that the Pocket Snatchers didn't learn their behavior on their own. This behavior was passed down from their parents, and in that case, the meeting would make no sense to even have. If you messed with the Pocket Snatchers they would jump on you; not only were the brothers, sisters, and cousins a part of this crew that would jump on you, the parents were as well. Matt was no push over and wasn't going to tolerate being bullied, but the headache and pestering wasn't worth it.

Lamar lived on Garfield Avenue with his mother and stepfather. He had a brother, as well as a sister, and was the oldest of the three. He probably had more siblings from his father's side, but that's something we never really touched base on. Even though Lamar's father wasn't in the picture much, he still had the presence of a father figure around. His stepdad was a successful lawyer, and he helped Lamar out the best way he could. He was there to teach Lamar right from wrong and to provide him with the proper guidelines it took to become a successful man. His parents were cool. His mother was beautiful and funny, and his stepdad would always have a story to make us laugh.

We all loved to hang out and sleep over his house playing video games and cracking jokes all night. This was our chill spot; in fact,

J.R. Smith from the Cleveland Cavaliers would stay over as well. It was like vacation when we were there, but when we went outside vacation was over. Reality kicked in. We were still in Jersey City and had to be prepared for whatever surprises these streets would have equipped for us on any given day.

There was a gas station just a few houses down from Lamar's house that would occasionally get robbed by gunpoint. Not to forget that he lived around the corner from the Pocket Snatchers and just a few blocks from the Smash Brothers. Also include the fact that at night certain parts of Garfield were pitch black if the street lights weren't functioning properly. An obstacle on top of obstacles. Jersey City was filled with nothing but dangerous obstacles.

Okay, so now there's a slight view on the different parts of the city we all grew up in. Problems varied in all of our parts, but basketball was our key goal. Basketball was our way out and that's all we wanted to do was play basketball. Eventually, basketball brought us all together and it was how we all actually met each other. Playing in CYO Leagues against each other and eventually coming together as one to play for the Boys & Girls Club of Jersey City.

We could play and play for days. We all had similar talents, could do pretty much the same things, and we played together so much that we began to feed off of each other. We knew what move the next person would do or what kind of pass he was going to make. We knew how to foul each other and how to get into each other's heads to throw one another's games off balance. We all became one, and nothing could have stopped us from progressing, or at least that's what we thought from the ages of 13-18. Little did we actually know; little did we know.

Sacred Heart CYO basketball team. Top row far left, Shelton Gibbs. Top row right side of the coach, Matthew Givens. Front row left side holding basketball, Ahmad Mosby.

INTERVIEW I

Question(Q): How was it growing up in Jersey City?
Beanie: *Rough, very rough. You had to deal with the streets, people coming after you on a day to day basis. Especially growing up with my family background. It was tough.*
Marcus: *Growing up in Jersey City was rough. There was a lot going on in the 90's, 2000's when we were kids. Me growing up in the projects, one of the toughest projects in Jersey City. You know, that was like one of the toughest things for me growing up.*
Otis: *For me, it wasn't too bad, but me being from the Hill I saw a lot of sheisty stuff. The only thing that kept me sane was basketball. I stayed in the courtyard all day long and distanced myself from a lot of the negative stuff. So I wasn't able to be into the negative things around me because I kept my ball in my hand.*

Q: What were some of the things you had to deal with coming from the area you came from?
Beanie: *Getting caught up into becoming a hustler. Then you had to deal with shootings, and it was just crazy. There was a lot going on. Too much!*
Marcus: *I had to deal with gun shots, crack fiends, and some of the toughest kids in the hood. You got to deal with all of that stuff. Walking in the projects every day, it was like you don't know if you're going to make it to your building or not. There was shit going on every day. There were people selling drugs 100 miles per hour. There were people coming down there shooting. You got to deal with the police. Me growing up in Curries Woods, you don't know what could have happened, from the youngest kid all the way to your grandmother.*
Otis: *I had to deal with fights, gunshots, drugs, and cops. That's just Jersey City you know. The same things go on everywhere in Jersey City. I wasn't in the projects, I'm in an open area where anything can come from anywhere. While you are playing ball in the park, it doesn't matter. No matter where you are in Jersey City, stuff still can happen.*

Q: Is there anything you wish you could have changed regarding where you grew up, things you saw, or problems you may have encountered?

Beanie: *Ummm, I wouldn't say so because it kind of made me who I am today. It made me take a different route and not want to take the negative route. Also, I could have gotten caught up with everything that was going on, but it made me think outside the box. Think that there was better things in life.*

Marcus: *The only thing I wish I could have changed for me personally was to have a father figure in my life. Other than that, everything I went through made me who I am today. So I wouldn't change shit!*

Otis: *Nah, I wouldn't change nothing. I wouldn't change anything at all. With everything that happened growing up, it prepared me to be strong for today.*

Q: How hard was it to not have your father in the picture as a kid? How did you feel? What were your thoughts at times?

Beanie: *That was hard. I had nobody to look up to. My brother was running the streets, all of my uncles were running the streets, cousins and some family members I didn't know about were running the streets. So, it was kind of like.* **(Paused)** *Who is there to show me the ropes? Like how to be a man, what's right, what's wrong, and all I had was my mother and sisters. They were always at work.*

Marcus: *That shit was tough for me. You know me growing up I didn't have nobody to come to my games. My mother wasn't at my games. I didn't really have the support everyone else was getting. Whether it was me playing baseball, basketball, football, it was tough. Me seeing your pops and mother come to things and other friend's parents. It was like, me, no parents. Not even my mother, and I don't even know my father. It was just like, I be wanting that shit. And it was crazy when all of us was growing up, like with you. You wanted to be out in the streets more, and I wanted to be in your shoes. It was like, nah man, cherish that shit because I don't even know my pops.*

Otis: *To be honest, I learned to live with it. I stopped getting mad. I stopped taking my anger out over stupid stuff. I just embraced your mother and father as my own. They embraced me as if I was theirs anyway. They yelled at me, just like they yelled* *at you. My mother had to work a lot. Working two jobs and taking care of two boys, she couldn't come to my games. My pops was somewhere driving trucks or I don't know. So after a while, it didn't really bother me.*

THE BOYS & GIRLS CLUB DAYS

BETWEEN THE AGES of 8-14 we would all run into each other at the Boys & Girls Club of Jersey City and compete against each other in the Club basketball leagues. Mostly all of us were playing for different teams at the time, but this would one day form our Boys & Girls Club Amateur Athletic Union (AAU) All-Star team. Marcus, Beanie, Milly, and I started playing for the AAU team between the ages of eight and ten. Milly, Beanie, and I were the younger three. A lot of the other Club guys were older than us but in the same grade as we were. They were held back because of the problems they encountered in school and it affected their grades. Sometimes preventing them from moving forward to the next grade level.

The Boys & Girls Club was our home away from home. If we weren't playing basketball, we would be in the game room or just hanging out at times. Shit at those ages we were young, full of energy, and would play basketball all day if we could. Yet the gym had to close, we had school the next day, and parents had to work. We didn't really notice at the time, but we were on the verge to becoming something bigger and better. Our AAU All-Star team would eventually go to win five State Championships in a row. Coaches came and went, players came and went, but our crew was there to stay.

Gary Greenburg was the man behind it all. He became like a father figure to all of us and took care of us when we needed. As we got older our team was progressing and getting better. We traveled back and forth to Orlando, Florida to play in the National AAU Tournament plenty of times ranking in the top twenty, but never reaching our goal of becoming number one in the nation. We had the heart and hunger to win the states every year because if we won we knew we would automatically qualify for the AAU National Tournament. Which meant we were going on a summer vacation. Our parents couldn't afford to send us on vacations every summer, so we found our way through basketball.

We started off playing for Derrick Mercer Sr. and Ike Ford at our young ages and things seemed to be good at the time. We were kids and we didn't pay any attention to grown-up things, so if the grown-ups had a problem we wouldn't notice them. It was strictly about basketball for us. Eventually the teams would get split up due to age difference and I would find myself bouncing between my age group and the older age group playing for both AAU teams.

I wanted to continue to play with Marcus and Matt because we all knew how to play with each other, but they were older. Beanie got to stay the course because they didn't have a guard at the age level above us and Beanie's skill level was definitely advanced. My team didn't have too many good players my age so I was basically forced to play with my age group to carry the team. I didn't mind because I would play the entire game, every game scoring 20 points or better.

Derrick Mercer Jr. was playing with us at the time and he was a good guard as well so we had leverage at two positions. Things seemed to be falling into place but one day something happened and there was a fall out with the grown-ups. We were kids and all we wanted to do was play basketball, so somehow they needed to get their shit together and patch things up. The next thing we knew Derrick Sr. and Ike Ford were gone. Gary told us that they were leaving, but not to worry he would find a new coach.

They left and created their own AAU team called the "Jersey City Heat." What the hell just happened? To us it seemed like with the snap of a finger things were just falling apart, but we didn't know what was going on behind closed doors. We didn't know how long the problems were going on or if there were even any problems at all. The only thing we knew was that we had no coach and lost several players because they went over to play for the Heat. It turned out that the teams being split up was actually because of this fallout.

Just as things seemed like they were hitting rock bottom and couldn't get any better, all of a sudden it flipped and things picked back up. We got more players and a new coach. Frank Burno would step forward as our coach and it all started picking back up. Corey Stokes joined the team who would later play for Villanova along with Derrick Caracter who ended up getting drafted and playing for the Los Angeles Lakers. We had a team now. Now we could get rid of whatever previous distractions we had going on and focus on our team, in my mind, my team.

Corey at the time was a younger player and he wasn't yet as polished of a player as I was, but he was on the verge to becoming one. His father and brothers were always on him, "Corey, shoot the ball and stop passing so much. Corey do this, and Corey do that," they would all say. They didn't let up on him and at times he seemed confused. At times, it seemed like it was too much on him and it would sometimes take him out of his game. They wanted Corey to be the star and try to do it all on his own, but I wasn't just going to be pushed to the side. I was tough, rough, and all over the place on the court. I took advantage of all the kids my age because I was too advanced for the players we played against.

I started to feel some type of way about Corey's father and how he was always on Corey. Always wanting him to jock and shoot the ball every play, so I sometimes stop passing the ball to Corey. He was about two years younger than me and he wasn't going to come on my team as a jock. He would learn to share or he wasn't getting the ball. At the end of the day the ball would end up in my hands first because most of the offensive plays were already designed for me.

I didn't know at first that Corey's brother was one of the coaches and I started bad mouthing Corey's father, not knowing it was his father as well. Boy, did that start a little dispute. Next thing you know I was meeting with his father and my father, but I didn't care at all because I was speaking the truth. I didn't have anything against Corey at all because I never saw him as a threat to my playing time. He was my friend and a cool kid.

However, I didn't like the fact that his father would tell him not to pass and to shoot all the time. That was my issue and my father understood where I was coming from. So after the little parent meeting, I didn't get in trouble for bad-mouthing Mr. Stokes because my dad saw it just like I did. Eventually things got patched up and we started to play as a team and it all came together. We became unstoppable and I would bounce back and forth from the 11-year-old AAU team to the 12-year-old AAU team.

When Derrick Caracter came to the Boys & Girls Club team he was playing baseball or soccer at the time. I remember going to his house with my father to basically recruit Derrick for the team. This kid was two years younger than me and fucking huge. He didn't really know how to play basketball but his size couldn't be ignored, he had to play basketball. Baseball and soccer were good sports, but basketball would fit this kid.

We got him over to the Boys & Girls Club and plenty of nights we would stay late to practice drills, just Derrick and me. I would help him with the drills he had problems with and he was picking up the sport fast. He became dominant and dominated every big man our age. We swept through the State Tournament that year beating all the teams and went to Florida for AAU.

I always wished that the older team didn't go to the National Tournament at the same time because I would sometimes get to travel with them as well if the National Tournament was a different week. I had the best of both worlds and I loved it. I wish the internet was as advanced back then as it is now because I would love to go back and look at our games just to reminisce, but all I can go off of is memory. The 12-year-old team was coming around but they were still missing a link to the chain. I was playing more for the 11-year-old team, so I wasn't around much to know what was going on.

We were about to begin a new AAU season and the 13-year-old team started practice first. Otis never played any form of organized ball and he was a great player. His skill level was too good for just playing ball in gym class and in the streets. I noticed that at my young age. While we were in 34 school, Otis begged me to bring him to the Boys & Girls Club to play on the team and it was so ironic that Coach Joe Whalen was looking for another player. I told Coach Whalen, who was a former St. Anthony coach, that I had the perfect player for the team. He told me he needed someone tall and he had to be good.

Otis was a slight bit taller than me at the time and I informed Coach Whalen that he would not be disappointed. When I got the news back to Otis he was excited, anxious, and focused. He loved ball and that's all he wanted to do. He finally got his chance to play for an AAU All-star team and he wasn't going to miss that at all. Coach Whalen wasn't disappointed when he saw Otis first touch the ball and I felt good about myself because I made this happen. They were both happy, the coach and Otis. In fact, Coach Whalen was so thrilled that any playing time that I was going to get was a dream short lived. I didn't mind because I still would play most of my minutes with the 12-year-old team.

At times, we would play back to back games. The 12-year-old AAU team followed by the 13-year-old AAU team and I would show out. I felt that Coach Whalen didn't think I was good enough to play with the other players so I would put on a show. It came easy to me, I could score when I wanted to and if I didn't score I was sent to the free throw line. Coach Whalen was watching and maybe it went unnoticed because of the skill level of my opponents, but I could play the same way with the kids a year older than me if he gave me the chance.

Still, when I switched that uniform and played the next level up, I didn't get much playing time. At first it didn't bother me because I just got finished playing an entire game, but as we moved on to high school and certain players left to other teams it became frustrating.

By the end of our eighth-grade year Gary was strongly encouraging all of us to attend St. Anthony High School. Marcus, Milly, Beanie, Matt, Otis, Lamar, and I were all heavily considering it already. It was the best basketball program in Jersey City and we didn't want to attend any other school. We wanted to play for the best coach and try to move forward. It was either St. Anthony or Marist High School. We all juggled back and forth deciding as a group, but we knew about the St. Anthony program. We figured this was our best option.

At home, my father sat me down and had a talk with me, he saw the bigger picture. He asked me what I thought about staying back a year and repeating the eighth-grade. At the time I thought this was ludicrous, there was no way in hell I was repeating the eighth-grade all over again. I felt I was good enough to play with everyone else even though I was 13 years old and the others were already 14 and 15 years old.

I told my father the only way I would repeat the eighth-grade was if I didn't have to do any work at all. I worked so hard to get good grades and move on to high school. Shit, he should have told me this at the beginning of the school year and I would have given the teachers a reason to keep me back. When he responded, and told me I would have to do work, I was turned off immediately by the idea.

Now this was probably a smart move for me to make and I didn't see it like that at the time. My age would have still allowed me to play basketball my senior year because I would still graduate at 18 years old. As Marcus, Otis, Beanie, Lamar, Milly, and Matt would be leaving their senior year; this would give me another year to shine and an even better chance to get recruited by big colleges. I see it now, but I didn't see it back then. I wish my father would have explained it better or just made me stay back instead of asking me. I would have been pissed off, but I will be damned if I wouldn't have gotten over it.

This was something that plenty of other talented players went through as they grew up. I wanted the challenge and I was just as good as they were. As long as I got the chance to shine I would make it happen, somehow, some way. I couldn't bear the thought of staying back in the eighth-grade and doing an extra year of school altogether. I hated school and the quicker I got out, the better. St. Anthony it was, and I would end up graduating at 17 years old.

Ohhh well!!!

We all went forward to St. Anthony High School except for Lamar who went to Marist High School, but still continued to play with the Boys & Girls Club. From 13 to 18 years old, we would go on to win five straight AAU State Championships. Coming close at times with the "Tim Thomas Playaz" who had players like J.R. Smith and Courtney Nelson, but we would still end up beating them for the AAU State Championships. Courtney played with us at the Boys & Girls Club but he left to go play for the Tim Thomas Playaz, so every game we played against him was personal. We thought he felt he was above all of us and we made sure we made his life hard on the basketball court.

J.R. Smith was a good friend of ours, but sometimes he and Matt would get into it on the court. They would get into it to the point they would almost fight. We had to break it up plenty of times between them. That was just an example of the type of player Matt was. He was a scrappy, rough player. He had his way of getting under your skin because he played good defense and would hound you. There were several times we got into fights on the court because of how Matt played.

We didn't only play AAU for the Club, we played in any tournament the Club ran. They held tournaments for the different teams around Jersey City and we found ourselves on the court fighting. Matt was getting under this players skin and we knew him, but he didn't know Matt.

While we were on the free throw line the kid turned to Marcus and said, "Yo tell your boy to chill out, he don't know me and I'm about to fuck him up." Well why did he say that? The next thing you know Matt turned and punched him in the face.

Now both of the teams rushed on the court and a brawl was underway. They squared up and another player was coming to blindside Matt, but our cousin Shawn caught him in the motion. "Down went Frazier, down went Frazier!" As they were still squared up I came over and butted into the fight punching the kid in the face. Otis and Beanie jumped on the other kids who were jumping in.

This all sprung out over the fact Matt got under this kid's skin on the basketball court. We were not known for backing down from anyone and we took basketball seriously, but took respect even more seriously. You were going to respect us on and off the court. If it was a fight you wanted, a fight you got. We didn't know any better. Fighting words were spoken and we didn't talk, we let our fighting skills do the talking. Win, lose, or draw we didn't care.

Our Boys & Girls Club basketball career was completely different from our St. Anthony career. We were different players for the Boys & Girls Club. We were ourselves. When we played for Coach Hurley we were actors and couldn't be ourselves. If someone said something smart to us we had to swallow our pride and let it go if it was a St. Anthony game, but if we were playing for the Club we got down and dirty with you.

We didn't know if Coach Hurley would hear the stories of the things we did while we played for the Boys & Girls Club. It was a different team and he wasn't there, so we didn't care. Until he said something to us about it, the behavior would continue and we would continue to be the rough and tough players we were.

After my freshman year at St. Anthony I received the MVP trophy for the freshman team. Matt and Beanie were also on the team with me so I just knew that Coach Whalen would see that I was a good player and I would get more time. Matt and Beanie were on the Boys Club team and got way more minutes than I did, but I was the one who got MVP for the St. Anthony freshman team. It wasn't handed to me, I earned it and it was definitely nothing against Matt and Beanie. I needed to prove a point to Coach Whalen that I could play as well.

I just knew I would get more time on the AAU team and practice was again under way. We were playing in the gym before practice started and I saw Coach Whalen walk into the gym. I started to pick up the pace just a little. I was on fire and every time I got the ball I would score. Otis knew I wanted to play more and I would tell him all the time so he kept passing me the ball. "Do your thing Ice, here take the ball" he said, and I continued to go off.

Between the legs, cross over, jump shot. Buckets!

In and out, cross over, layup. Buckets!

Post move, fake right, go left, shot fake, watch the defensive player jump in the air like a fool. Buckets!

All this time I noticed that Coach Whalen was watching and I saw the surprised look on his face. He looked as if he never even noticed I could play this way. Before we started practice he even said to me, "Shelton you got better, you've been working hard." This motivated me and I just knew my time would increase, and it did. I got 30 more seconds on the court. What the hell was going on? I couldn't understand and it got to the point where I didn't even care anymore. Let me just stick around and go on the trips were my thoughts.

The end of our junior year going into senior year in high school, our AAU team was beginning to wind down. This was basically the last year we could play AAU basketball before we moved onto college. None of us really noticed this at first, we really didn't realize the transition we would have to make the next year until it was actually over.

Still, I had hopes of getting more playing time. My junior year in high school I was one of the starting five players at St. Anthony for half the season. I just knew Coach Whalen would take that into consideration. I mean I had to have some kind of talent that the best high school coach in the world gave me a chance to be a part of the starting five half the season. With the little hopes that I had, that didn't mean shit to Coach Whalen. I assume he had his favorites and that was completely fine with me. I couldn't take it personally; Coach Whalen was a great guy at the end of the day. He listened to us, he cared.

Ahmad Nivins was sent over to our AAU team to play with us and we were hard on him at first. We showed him tough love because we wanted him to get better. He was tall and still didn't fully have basketball down pat, but he damn sure would get it down pat playing with us. We didn't take it easy on him one bit. He had no choice but to become a strong player and a strong person because we got under his skin. He got stronger, he got better, and soon we left him alone. Ahmad was now a part of our group.

We went to Las Vegas to play in a tournament and the week after we were heading to play in the AAU tournament. When we got to Las Vegas we were smacked in the face with a surprise. Something went wrong with Coach Whalen's registration as the coach of the team, so we didn't have a coach. Ryan Whalen, his son, who was our teammate ended up being a player/coach.

Now we were out in Las Vegas playing basketball and our real coach couldn't even sit on the bench with us. He had to sit in the stands as a fan. We were fucked! Coach Whalen explained to us that he wanted us to have fun and that this wasn't all that important, but the AAU tournament was. We saw it his way because at the end of the day we were in Las Vegas baby. He didn't have to tell us to have fun because we definitely were going to have some fun.

We played our first game and struggled at first from jet lag but picked it up and ended up winning. When night came we hit the Las Vegas strip. He told us to stay together, to be safe, and we had a ball. Ahmad stood about six feet seven inches tall towering over everyone we walked by and holding his camcorder videotaping everything.

A limo driver drove past us and beeped his horn, the next thing we knew he stopped. We all ran over to the limo and he told us to hop in, he would give us a free limo ride around town. This was the life, 17 and 18 years old driving around Las Vegas in a limo. You couldn't tell us shit.

Before we knew it, it was about 3 o'clock in the morning and we found ourselves in MGM Grand. We were trying to get someone to buy us some liquor. Yeah, we were under age, but we were going to spice it up some. The guy came out of the store and told us that they weren't able to buy the liquor. The next thing we knew, MGM Grand Metro grabbed Matt and me.

They took us in the basement of MGM and made us sit until we called an adult to pick us up. Now Matt and I are locked in this basement and all we could think is Coach Whalen was going to kill us. They called Coach Whalen who was sleep in his room and he got to us around 4 o'clock in the morning. I gave the Metro Police a completely fake name and Matt gave them a fake last name. We didn't know what we were doing, but if they had names on file they weren't going to have our real names.

Coach Whalen laughed at us and said, "I told you guys to have fun not get arrested, who was trying to buy the liquor?" Of course we lied, "Coach it wasn't us." Come to find out, the guy we asked to buy us liquor went into the liquor store and told on us. The Metro Police had no idea it was us at all. They told us that some kids were trying to buy liquor and they ran off while we happened to be in the wrong place at the wrong time.

We took the story and ran with it because we were actually the kids they were talking about. Everyone else ran while Matt and I were grabbed up. We were surprised that Coach Whalen didn't scream, yell, or even make us go in our rooms. We had a game at ten in the morning and it was now five in the morning. He told us not to stay out much longer and to get to the game on time.

We met back up with the others and they laughed at us the rest of the morning. We had the time of our lives and so much fun. This was

Ahmad's first time on a trip with us and we all had a blast. He got to see the things we did and what we were like, he fit right in. We played the next day tired as hell and I think we even lost the game, but I don't remember. The only thing that was important was that we were having fun and like Coach Whalen said, the AAU National Tournament was all that really mattered.

From Vegas, we took a flight straight to Orlando, Florida. We left the fun and games in Las Vegas, because we all know, "What happens in Vegas, stays in Vegas," and we brought our game faces to Florida. No staying out until five in the morning or running around late, it was game time. We won our first game easily and anyone who is familiar with the AAU National Tournament or any other Tournament knows that it doesn't get easier as you move forward. The next few games got tougher but we were sticking it out win after win.

We finally got to the point where we were playing against Ronald Glen (Big Baby) Davis, who was drafted to the Seattle Sonics from Louisiana State. Shortly after he was traded to the Boston Celtics, then to the Orlando Magic. If we won this game we would have one more game left to get to the AAU National Championship and if we lost we would have to play for fifth place.

We were excited and anxious to win. The game started off close and in our favor. David Whitehurst, who went to the University of Pennsylvania played on our AAU team and was having a field day. He was hot, Beanie was hot, Otis was hot, everybody was on their A-game. Yet this team was having the same kind of streak and Glen Davis was astonishing. He was all over the court standing about six feet five inches tall, and if he wasn't all over he seemed like he was. Point guard, shooting guard, small forward, he was doing it all.

We ended up losing the game and it crushed us but we played our hardest which was all that mattered. If we would have won, we would be set to play against Al Ricardo Jefferson who went pro out of high school to the Boston Celtics. He would move on to play for the Minnesota Timberwolves and the Utah Jazz.

We placed fifth place and our AAU careers were officially over, it was then that we noticed this was our last year playing AAU ball ever. It never really dawned on us until we were on the way home. The years and years of AAU basketball starting from 8 years old was officially over, but we still had one more season left at St. Anthony.

Marcus seemed to change after this tournament. Out of all of us I think that he was the only one who really noticed what was coming for the future. His life was basketball and Marcus's basketball IQ was an A+. Marcus saw something and when we got back home he let us all know he had something to say. When we landed and gathered our belongings he simply told us that he was tired of this shit.

"We have one more season left at St. Anthony and that shit is not going to end like our Boys & Girls Club career did." That's all Marcus said and those of us that were on the team understood.

Boys & Girls Club travel team. Top row far left, Marcus Williams. Top Row Center, Ahmad Mosby. Center row far left, (half covered) Jameel George. Center row left center, Derrick Mercer. Center row far right, Shelton Gibbs.

Boys & Girls Club travel team. Back row far left, Jameel George. Back center left, Marcus Williams. Back center right, Shelton Gibbs. Front row left of center player, Derrick Mercer. Front row right of center player, Ahmad Mosby.

Boys & Girls Club travel team. Far left, Ahmad Mosby. Back center right looking towards camera, Jameel George. Front center looking towards the left, Shelton Gibbs.

Boys & Girls Club travel team. Center, Ahmad Mosby. Far right, Shelton Gibbs.

INTERVIEW II

Q: What does the name Gary Greenburg mean to you?
Beanie: *G-Man!* ***(Laughing)*** *That's the man right there! Gary is the man! It all started with him bringing me down to the Boys & Girls Club. I was playing in the summer league with the older guys and he discovered me. Then from there on he has been a close friend.*
Marcus: *Gary Greenburg, that name means a lot you know. He kind of put me towards the right direction. He helped me out with AAU Basketball and traveling. Instead of being in the streets he told me,* ***"You're a good kid, come and play for the Boys & Girls Club."*** *He took me to a lot of places that I probably would have never been to. Florida, Disney World. He is a great guy and he helped me out in a tremendous way.*
Otis: *Gary Greenburg to me is like something that came out of the blue. I don't have nothing bad ever to say about Gary. He came to my grammar school to make sure I was good. He granted me the opportunity to travel at a very young age. He just really looked out for me personally. He didn't have to do that.*

Q: What role did the Boys & Girls Club and Gary Greenburg play in your decision to attend St. Anthony High School?
Beanie: *A big role! Where else was I going to go? Let's be honest. Playing at the Boys Club, there was no other outlet in Jersey City if you wanted a better life. Especially being an athlete playing basketball. So it was no other option. I was going to St. Anthony.*
Marcus: *The Boys Club, Gary, and St. Anthony has a long-term connection. All the inner-city kids from Jersey City that St. Anthony had playing mostly started at the Boys & Girls Club. Gary Greenburg recognized a lot of stars just from all the Housing Authorities going to the Club and playing basketball. That had a big role for me and my decision to go to St. Anthony. It was like tradition. Gary took care of me and he liked St. Anthony. So that's where my loyalty stood.*

Otis: *There was no such thing as of what role. You going to St. Anthony period! Ain't no debating about it.* **(Laughing)** *You are playing for the Club, you good, it's not up for debate. That's where you are going. I didn't dispute it. I was hyped to go to St. Anthony.*

Q: Otis, I remember in elementary school, you begged me to bring you to the Boys & Girls Club so you can play basketball with the team. How did you feel when I brought you to the Club and Coach Whalen wanted you to play?

Otis: *Word up!* **(Laughing)** *And I took your spot! I felt happy as hell. I felt like I had something to do after school. I ain't have to play outside with nowhere to go. Now I felt like I had something to play for. That was like my real first team I ever played on. I was at your house an hour before we were supposed to go to the Club. I was hyped!*

Q: Otis, do you think you would have ended up at St. Anthony if you never played for the Club?

Otis: *Nope! Nobody would have ever saw me. I would have been a star talent that never went anywhere. Just a city player. Outside player not really known at the national level. Getting exposure! Being on T.V.! Being in the newspaper! None of that! I would have been a waste of time and talent. The Boys Club changed my life. Basically.*

Q: What was it about the Boys Club team that was so special?

Beanie: *We was a family! That's what kept us together. That's what kept us close. And then winning. We had so much fun just winning. Just beating everybody. It was the life.*

Marcus: *We all had the same motives. We all grew up in Jersey City less than five to ten minutes in the same areas. So we all was motivated to just make it. We played together as one and never looked at each other as to who is better than who. We*

played as brothers. We had that bond that there was nothing you can take from that. We had the chemistry year in and year out. The best thing was that we was together.
Otis: *We played so long together, we knew each other. I know if I had a steal and Marcus was behind me, it's going off the backboard. If I have a fast break going to the hole, I can kick it out to Beanie for three. Lamar playing defense like crazy or you trying to dunk on everybody. Me, I'm just the star like I always am.* **(Laughing)** *We just knew each other. We never had no egos on the team. That's why we never went to the Playaz. That was the thing, nobody could break us. No matter what they did or what they said. Nobody could break us. Still to this day I feel the same way.*

Q: Marcus, when our Boys & Girls Club careers were over, we had one last season at St. Anthony. You told us you were tired of the shit and that our St. Anthony career was not going to end the same way. What was going through your mind when you said that?
Marcus: *With me, I'm competitive! So it was more like I hate to lose. When we lost that last game, we was playing against Big Baby who went to the NBA. I knew we had the talent and the hunger to win. It was just like, we are going to get over the hump and I didn't like that losing feeling. So the same hunger and motivation I know we had, I wanted it to carry over to St. Anthony and for us not to turn back.*

LIVING IN JERSEY CITY

THE STREETS WERE right in front of us; no matter where we went, or what we did, we would have to deal with the trials and tribulations that came along with living in Jersey City. Now we all came from different areas but word would travel through the city quicker than the strike of lightening. If there was a fight on the opposite side of town you knew about it. You knew who was involved, what it was over, and the ending results. Childhood into young adulthood we would all face difficulties coming up in Jersey City. You never had to be the one to start the trouble, no don't worry about that, because trouble would have its way of finding you.

As elementary school kids, we would have to fight to protect ourselves or to make sure that we weren't being bullied. Therefore, you would have to make an example out of the school bully just to make sure he knew to stay away from you. Who would think we would have to worry about someone having a knife, maybe even someone pulling a gun out and scaring you into giving up your personal belongings? These were the things we would eventually have to deal with, come face to face with, and we weren't even teenagers.

A suburban kid would be scared as shit if he or she spent one day in a Jersey City public school, or even on the streets of Jersey City because they would be introduced to an environment they never knew existed. This wasn't the lifestyle that we necessarily wanted; this was the lifestyle that our parents could afford and we had to make the best of it.

As seventh and eighth-graders, we all probably looked like we were older than what we actually were. So when we would play basketball around the neighborhood, the other kids would tend to think we were high school kids. Maybe the fact that we all probably lied about our ages at some point in our lives to impress the older girls would play a role in it as well. Matt, Otis, Lamar, and Marcus were a year or two older than Milly, Beanie, and me. We were around 11 and 12 years old and they were already 13 and 14 years old going on 15 years old. They were old enough to be in high school but still in elementary school.

Now it would seem to be something outside of the norm, but in all of our schools we had kids that were 14 or 15 years old in the eighth-grade. In our eyes, this was the norm and we didn't know anything else. I was in the seventh and eighth-grade with a class full of kids that were 14, 15, and 16 years old. These kids had already experienced their first encounter with drugs, alcohol, and sex. At our young ages, we were introduced to these things and the peer pressure was strong. It was so strong that Lamar fathered his first child while we were in the eighth-grade. Even though Lamar was one of the older ones, it was still a very young age to become a father. Not to use Lamar as an example, but this was just one type of obstacle that we had to worry about growing up.

As kids, we would play basketball at any playground we could play at and sometimes it wasn't the smartest idea. I remember playing basketball in the courtyard of my elementary school one day and this kid that was in high school came and started to play. Now he wasn't a high school kid that played high school ball. He was one of those high school kids that swore up and down they were good at ball, but could never make the team because he didn't have the dedication to stick through tryouts. Instead of being dedicated to going to tryouts and learning the sport, he was more dedicated to hanging out in the streets.

Anyway, we were playing ball and I did a cross over that made him stumble. The other kids laughed and sighed which pissed him off. Now at

16 years old this kid was starting a fight with a 12-year-old. I told him I didn't want to fight, but all of these kids were encouraging him to punch me in my face. At 12 years old, I was the same size as him and even more physically built than he was, but I was scared because he was older than me. However, I knew one thing, if this kid punched me in my face I was going to kick his ass or even try my best to. I didn't get punched that day. Maybe it was because of my size or the fact that I told him I was 12 years old and he was 16 years old, but regardless he didn't punch me.

A few weeks would pass since my run in with this high school kid. One of my friends was being bullied by a kid I knew from his earlier years in our elementary school. He was another kid that was 14 or 15 years old in the seventh-grade and there was some kind of program that passed which would allow him to be pushed up to high school. He was coming back to the school and bullying one of my close friends and I couldn't stand bullies. I asked him several times to stop bullying my friend because he was scared, but he wouldn't stop.

We eventually got into a fight squaring up outside of the school. I thought of fighting like I was on the basketball court. Fake left, go right, straight jab, score! Stutter step, watch which way the opponent moves for an open hit, score! Just so happened he was friends with the kid I played basketball with a few weeks earlier. After our first fight and him being whooped on you would think this kid would leave me alone. Instead he went to get his friends and we squared up for a second fight within an hour later. I lunged at him and he buckled up so I told him I wasn't fighting him because it was unfair. As I turned to walk away, directly behind me was this kid from the basketball court. I bumped into him and this gave him a reason to want to fight me.

My friend's brother told me to come in the house because I was outnumbered and all of my other friends had gone home, but I wasn't going in the house. I told him I would be fine and continued to walk the three blocks it would take for me to get home. Now a crowd of guys and girls were walking behind me, some I knew and some I didn't know, and this kid was right beside me along with his buddies. I finally got to the point where I stopped and asked him what it was he wanted to do. He looked away from me and when he turned back he was throwing his fist at me.

Oh, but I saw that fist coming and moved.

I hit this kid so hard that he fell on me and it seemed as if he was just laying on me sleeping, but I didn't stop hitting him. The next thing you know I was blindsided and sucker punched. My adrenaline wouldn't let the hit phase me. I then hit the other kid to get him out of the way. These kids were jumping me and I was getting the best of all of them. My girlfriend at the time was raised in a house full of brothers and she would wrestle with her brothers all the time. So as I would hit one kid off of me, she would grab him and throw him to the sidewalk. The fight would eventually end, but my day was still far from over.

An hour later my friend Jamel (Daly) Graham rang my bell, he was outside with a group of my other friends and they heard about what happened. He informed me that everyone was around the corner and they were waiting. I could now fight this kid again but this time everyone would make sure it was a fair fight. I was exhausted, but I knew if I didn't go to fight I would hear it the next day in school. You had to be tough and if you weren't tough you were like a target. I refused to be a target for anyone. So, I came back outside and walked around the corner to my third fight.

There must have been a total of 20 to 30 kids outside and it was again time to fight. This fight started off bad for me. I just wanted to get it over with so I threw a punch that had no chance of even landing, but if it did the fight probably would have been over. He ducked down, picked me up, and slammed me. He never got to hit me while I was down because I was sticking and moving. Even though he had me on my back, I made it very hard for him to hit me and after punching the concrete a few times he decided to get up. The fight was over but this was definitely not our last encounter with each other.

When my father came home, my mother told him I was outside fighting and the lump on my face from when I got blindsided told him the rest. He asked me what happened, I explained and I wished it was over from there but he took me to look for the guys I was fighting. I already had a long day and now my father was taking me back outside to look for the guys I was fighting so we could make peace with each other. I didn't want to make peace at all and I was hoping they weren't even outside. It would be something embarrassing and little did my father know it would be the reason I would probably have to fight again.

They labeled me as a snitch and word got around fast. We were raised by the rule that snitching wasn't cool and the famous saying "Snitches Get Stitches." My father was a Probation Officer and everyone considered that as being a Police Officer. These kids weren't happy with that, and I wasn't going to back down. Matt and Milly found out about this and they came around my area for the entire following week. That entire week we went around looking for the kid and we ended up crossing paths at the end of the week. We were prepared to fight and that's exactly what I wanted to do, fight, but the kid had other intentions.

I think he knew I would keep coming back and we would keep fighting every time we saw each other. Without any presence of an adult around he did something that surprised me. He came up to me along with his friends and we really made peace out of the situation. From there my name was cleared. It's hard to be labeled as a snitch because you never know who would see you as a threat and end up wanting to harm you. I was sure glad it was cleared because I didn't want those problems, but if push came to shove I would be prepared.

Around the seventh and eighth-grade is when the fighting started, at least for me that was. Milly and Marcus grew up in the projects so fighting was something that was expected of them. In Curries Woods, you were taught to take your differences to the park and handle them there. The winner would be the first one who walked out because they had whooped on the other so bad it took them a little longer to get up and get out of the park.

There was a street gangster by the name of "Dee Bo" may GOD rest his soul, who ran the projects back then. The entire Jersey City knew about Dee Bo and boy was he a force to be reckoned with. Growing up in the projects, if your projects fought any outsiders and you didn't help, Dee Bo made sure when you got back to the projects you were considered lunch meat.

Yup, lunch meat to be fed to the wolves because you would learn to stand by your projects and fight. Not fighting was nowhere near an option for Marcus and Milly, fighting was a must. Even if they didn't want to fight they couldn't show it because it proves them to be weak and it was like this in all of our areas. We became immune to a life that we didn't necessarily want to become immune to, but we really had no choice.

When I was 11 years old, I witnessed something that an 11-year-old should never witness. I was at a very close friend's house at the time spending the night. My friend Ryan, his older brother Shawn, and I were sitting on the porch late at night eating ice cream. Out of nowhere a guy comes sprinting past the house. I swore this guy was a track star and as he ran by I thought to myself, man this guy is fast. I quickly found out the reason he was in a rush and I could only hope that his speed paid off this night.

Within seconds of him sprinting by us, three guys in all black ran and stopped right in front of us. One guy pulled out a hand gun and pointed it at him. As he pointed the gun he yelled out, "I got him!" The second guy pulled out a hand gun and yelled, "No! I got him!" All of our eyes widened open as if we just saw ghosts and it wasn't over just yet.

The third guy reached in his jacket and pulled a shotgun out. "Move! Move! Move! I got him!" He racks the slide and fires the shotgun.

BOOM!

Ryan and I are sitting there in shock. Shawn grabs us and yells, "Get in the house! Get in the house!" Scrambling, we both get up and run in the house as Shawn slams the front door shut and locks it.

Running up the stairs, we heard nothing but gun shots. We didn't know if that guy got away safely, but whatever he did to piss them off didn't seem like it would end well for him. If he did get out of that situation, he had better change his life around and change it fast. This was my very first encounter with gun violence, and it wouldn't be the last.

We played in basketball leagues in all the local areas to stray away from all the violence, but sometimes the violence still caught up to you. It was like that annoying person that you couldn't get rid of and he/she would always somehow find you. Public School #38 ran basketball leagues that all the public schools and private schools were invited to play in. Otis, Lamar, and I were playing for St. Paul's basketball team and his stepfather was coaching us at the time. After the game he offered to give me a ride home. I had a few friends there and my cousin Shawn, so I wanted to walk because we couldn't all fit in the car. They came to watch me play so I figured I would walk with them being that they lived in the same area. We got to my block and parted ways.

In the day time, my street was like a block party, full of kids and parents outside having a good time. Yet come night, it was quiet and dark. I never really had any problems, but that wasn't the case this night. I heard footsteps coming from behind me and quickly assumed that one of my friends was running up on me to play around or something.

As I turned around, I saw a shiny chrome object pointed to my face. It was way too fast for this not to be my friends playing games with me, so I told the gunman to stop playing thinking it was one of my buddies. I was shocked that one of my friends had a gun and was waving it in my face, telling me to take off my jacket. At least that is what was going through my mind. I was only 12 years old at the time and never really came face to face with a gun before. The only time I ever saw one was a year ago sitting on Ryan's porch.

However, this was not a game and neither was this a friend of mine. My eyes were so focused on the gun that I didn't realize this guy had his face covered and not too far behind him was a few more guys coming with their faces covered.

I saw a taxi driver that just dropped off someone to their home and I screamed for help, but the taxi driver sped off. I was running out of time because the other guys were catching up. All I knew was that it was cold outside and this was a brand-new coat that I wasn't ready to give up. I figured I would be shot because in the movies every time someone pulled a gun out they would shoot somebody. I wasn't ready to be shot at 12 years old, so the only thing that came to my mind was to somehow get the gun out of this guy's hand.

I grabbed his wrist and the gun at the same time and gave it a good twist. I twisted his wrist so hard that he basically gave me the gun, but the other guys were right there. I didn't know what else to do so I pushed the guy with all my might and ran. I was the fastest person on earth that night, and all I was thinking was don't look back and don't fall. My house wasn't too far and all I had to do is make it to my father, he would protect me.

A gunshot rang out, and the car's window that was next to me shattered. Another gunshot rang out after another. My boots slipped off my feet but I wasn't stopping. I looked up and saw my father in the window from hearing the gun shots, and my father saw me. I don't know if I took a breath at all, but when the shots stopped I turned around and the robbers were running the opposite way.

"Whooaa, I was lucky!!!"

My dad rushed outside half naked and asked me several times if I was shot. "Shelt, are you shot? Shelt, are you shot?" I couldn't answer, I needed to catch my breath. "No dad, I'm fine" was my response, "let me go and get my boots." He was furious. He asked me what happened and I explained to him they were trying to rob me for my jacket. He then asked me why I didn't give it to them. Now in my mind I'm saying, "Shit its cold as hell outside, they weren't getting this jacket," but my mouth simply said I wasn't giving up my new jacket.

He sat me down and said "Son, let me explain something to you. I know that you just got this jacket and you like it a lot, but the next time if there is a next time, please just give the jacket up. I can buy you a brand-new jacket even better than the one you have on now, but I can't buy you a new life." That statement made all the sense in the world and it was 100% right.

The cops showed up and I had to run them through the entire situation all over again. The taxi driver told them he saw the robbery and followed the kids around the corner, but how could that be true when the taxi driver took off when I called for help. I was confused, tired, and looking at a book of pictures that didn't make sense for me to look at because I didn't see a face at all. All I saw was the barrel of that gun and the sounds of the gunshots continuously replaying in my head.

We drove around in the back of the cop car looking for the robbers for about two hours and I couldn't figure out why because I didn't see anyone's face. After we got back home, my father suggested I stay home from school. No way, I had a competition in gym class the next day that I needed to win and take a test I needed to pass. So I told him to forget about it I'm going to school, let me take another day off.

In school the next day, I was called over the intercom and told to report to the principal's office. Now in my mind I'm thinking, "What did I do? Damn I should have just stayed home like my father told me to." I guess my father told them what happened and they brought in a psychologist to talk to me and see what was going on in my head. I told myself I was fine and I didn't need to talk with anyone, and I guess the psychologist felt the same way when I spoke to her because she never came back to talk to me.

Little did I know that a kid from school saw me in the back of the cop car the night before and thought I had been arrested. Now I had a rumor going on through the school that I was arrested last night which was completely not true and I explained to my classmates what happened. One of them thought it was funny and he laughed, made jokes, and teased at me. I knew I couldn't get to him in the class because I would probably get suspended but I wanted to choke the shit out of him. I got my chance when he asked for that pass to the bathroom though, because I asked for a pass right with him.

As soon as we walked in the bathroom I grabbed him and put him in a headlock. I don't know what came over me but I kept asking him was he the one who tried to rob me last night. Over and over I asked him and he repeatedly said no. I realized I quickly snapped and when I let him go this kid had urinated in his pants. I guess he got what he deserved because when we went back to class he was the one on the end of all the jokes. Now he had to call his mommy into school to bring him a change of clothes, and I heard no more jokes from him.

It took me a few weeks to get over what happened and for a while I never walked home again or wore my favorite coat. The only way to get over your fear was to face it and I eventually started to walk home again. I got a BB gun and took the orange tip off which was a very dangerous thing to do and I realize it now, but back then I didn't care I just knew it would protect me.

Things must really work out in mysterious ways because a few months later walking down my block in broad daylight, I was face to face with another situation. A man in a red car pulled up and told me to come to his car, waving for me to come and get in. It was day time and there were a lot of people outside. My neighbors asked me if I knew him. They saw the look on my face and noticed something was wrong. I was so scared that I couldn't even talk; all I could do was shake my head no when they asked.

I had my BB gun tucked in my pants but I couldn't pull it out while the neighbors were on their porches. The guy kept following me and followed me around the corner where he parked to get out of the car. I slowed down and I was now out of sight of my neighbors, but I was prepared. I didn't have a real gun, but boy I knew those BB's would hurt. When he opened the door to get out of the car he was huge. There was no way this man was catching me in a foot chase from the distance we were apart. He smiled and I knew this man wanted to take me. GOD only knows what he wanted to do, but it wasn't happening this day.

I pulled out the BB gun and pointed it at him when he got to the back of his car. The look on his face was completely priceless and I felt in a position of power now. He was no longer smiling. The BB gun looked so real and I was glad I had it this day or I probably would have ended up on one of those milk cartons as a missing child.

He put his hands up and started to back up to his door. Now I never shot this BB gun before and I thought it wouldn't be loud, but this BB gun was just as loud as a real gun. I fired the first BB and it bust out his tail light. He tried to run so fast but he was huge and his body wouldn't allow him to move too quickly. I fired another BB and he was in the door speeding off.

GOD was with me once again.

You never knew what kind of tricks the streets of Jersey City had up its sleeves, but you can always guarantee that the surprise might be one that would end you up in trouble. Things would only get worse growing up in this city and as we all moved forward to high school, we would all encounter more dangerous and near-death experiences. However, this is where we lived and there was nothing we could do about it. None of us were the type of kids to just sit in the house. That was too boring. We liked to ride our bikes around town, hang out with girls, and play basketball.

As teenagers, we never thought negative because we were young and we didn't have the wrong intentions on our minds at all. All we wanted to do was have fun and when it was time to play ball we would put on our game faces. We would play ball wherever, whenever, and however anyone wanted to play.

After a day of hanging out Marcus was at my house and decided to walk home. Curries Woods was a far walk from my house and my parents weren't home to give him a ride, so he decided to walk home until he saw a bus he could jump on. We slapped hands and Marcus was on his way.

Within an hour later I received a call from Marcus who was very excited, upset, and screaming. "Yo, I just got robbed Shelt," he said. I couldn't believe it and in my mind, I'm thinking was someone following us the entire time and watched him as he left my house? What was going on? After asking myself all of these questions, I then asked Marcus what happened and he began to explain. As he was walking down Ocean Avenue getting closer to home, a car full of guys drove by him. He noticed the car but being that they kept going he really didn't pay them any attention.

When he got to the corner, the car and the guys were waiting for him. One of the guys approached him with a gun while the others grabbed him up. The gunman told him not to move or he will be shot and all Marcus could do was sit there hoping nothing would happen to him. They went through all of his pockets. Any jewelry he had on, any money, or anything of value he had was theirs to keep. They even took his monthly bus pass his mother purchased for him to be able to get back and forth to school.

This gave me flashbacks to a few years earlier when I was 12 years old and all I could remember was what my dad told me. I reiterated that speech to Marcus but in my own words. I told him he was lucky because he could have been shot and he did the right thing by giving up his belongings. It was the end of the month anyway, he would get a new bus pass in a few days. He was on the phone able to talk to me, when he could have been a body in the streets outlined in chalk and having his death investigated. I explained all of this to him and he was still mad, but it eased his mind a little. All he could say to me in the end was, "Shelt you are absolutely right."

These were the things we had to deal with every day and it became annoying. We couldn't hang out without worrying if someone would bother us, which would cause us to end up fighting, or if someone would ride up on us and pull a gun out to rob us. Who was I to tell Marcus he did the right thing by giving up his belongings? Was it even the right thing to do?

The right thing to do is helping people when you see them struggling with something. If you saw that someone dropped something and didn't notice they dropped it, you pick it up and return it to them because that's the right thing to do. What made it right for him to give up his belongings to someone that put a gun in his face? Was it right because it would save his life? Because it definitely wasn't right for the guys to rob him!

I was tired of the nonsense and I didn't know what to do. The only thing I could think of was something that was completely wrong. I decided to purchase a gun, not a BB gun, a real gun. No one would be robbing us anymore, no one would bother us anymore, and no one would want to fight us because we would all have protection when we walked the streets of Jersey City. If we wanted to play basketball we would play basketball where we wanted to. If we rode our bikes we would be protected because I now had protection for all of us. I let this be known to all of the guys and they thought I was crazy, but we all felt a little safer to walk the streets.

I wasn't at all a bad kid nor was I raised to be a bad kid. There was too much going on and I was tired of my friends and me ending up on the wrong side of the fence. I didn't carry the gun everywhere I went; I hid it good from my parents so they would never find it. I didn't plan on shooting anyone, I knew what the consequences would be if I did that. I brought it to scare people away, the robbers. If any of my friends wanted the gun to walk home, they could get it with no problem. We were safe!

I was cool with one of Marcus's cousins and I used to hang out on Dwight Street in Jersey City with a few guys I grew up with in elementary school. We went to different high schools now but time to time I would come around the block and hang out in the Public School #15 court yard. Trouble once again found its way of coming around one night. This time it was Marcus's cousin that would have the honor, or should I call it the horror. He recently had a fight with a crew of kids from another area in the city and they were coming back for revenge this night.

Now something wasn't right at all with how they came around because there was a good 30 of us outside playing football and riding bikes. They pulled up in a car with four people. Who in their right state of mind would pull up to fight someone that's hanging around at least 29 other kids? However, they did and Marcus's cousin felt confident and walked towards the car. I grabbed him and told him not to go to the car because something wasn't right. "Why would they pull up to a crew of people with only four people in their car?" I asked him and he didn't care. He snatched his arm away from me then proceeded to the car. Him and 28 others rushed to the car while I sat back on my bike and watched.

Common sense told me something wasn't right and I hit it right on the money. A gunshot went off and the crowd quickly scattered. Marcus's cousin was still at the car scuffling with one of the kids and it came by surprise to me that a female had the gun in her hand. She fired a shot in the air to get rid of the crowd and she definitely got rid of them. Once the crowd dispersed, Marcus's cousin was the only one around the four.

They came for blood that night because one of the guys snatched the gun and shot him. I saw him laid out in the street. My heart was racing and I was too far for them to get to me. I hoped they didn't notice who I was, then they got back in the car and sped away. I rode my bike up to him and he was bleeding from his head. He should have listened to me, if only he would have listened.

I quickly jumped on my Nokia cell phone to call 911. I told them I just saw my friend get shot in the head and to come fast. He was still breathing because I could hear him snoring on the ground as if he was sound asleep. I told the dispatcher all I could. I stayed until I heard the ambulance coming and then rode off on my bike.

I wasn't sticking around to talk to the police, because if I did that I felt I would become a target. No way was I being approached and watching my back every day. I just saw them shoot my friend and if they shot him, what would stop them from coming after me to shoot me for telling on them? I didn't quite see their faces because I was far, but I saw the car. Maybe this could have helped the police, but I didn't want to take the chance of becoming the target of a hit man.

When I got home I called Marcus and told him his cousin had been shot and I saw the entire thing. He was fuming and he understood that I couldn't tell the police about what I saw. The next day he told me his cousin was still alive and the bullet grazed through the front of his cousin's head. It was a big sigh of relief because I just knew his cousin was on the floor dying. He told me his cousin was in a coma and the doctors said they would have to closely monitor him, but was unsure as to whether his condition would improve. A few weeks later he was out of the coma and we were just happy to find out that he was going to be okay.

We were high school kids and it was hard dealing with the everyday issues in the streets and now dealing with the very high demanding rules of our basketball coach, Coach Bob Hurley. He didn't know everything we were going through at home and what issues we had going on. Maybe if he did, he wouldn't have been so hard on us. Truth be told, he probably felt he needed to be hard because we would carry over our frustrations into school and sometimes on the court. We became the product of our environments and we had this rough swagger about us.

We couldn't talk to Coach Hurley about these things; even if we could we were scared to. Our parents were hard working parents; they were doing everything they could do. We felt we had to take certain situations in our own hands and that's exactly what we did. We dealt with the streets the way we knew how and we dealt with Coach Hurley on the other hand. He was the least of our problems and when he yelled at us we became numb to it; in one ear and out of the other.

Don't get me wrong, Coach Hurley taught us a lot and was there for us. Yet sometimes we weren't fully focused. In the gym with Coach Hurley was one thing, but when we left to go and catch the bus home was a different worry. Basketball was on our minds 20%, 5% girls, and the other 75% was spent worrying about our safety or what could happen in the streets on our way home from practice.

Problem after problem would arise in high school and we dealt with the problems the best way we could and the quietest we could. We had to keep our street life separate from school, basketball, our parents, and Coach Hurley. We weren't being rebels or starting trouble and keeping that a secret. We didn't want our parents to know that sometimes we fought because they would probably force us to make peace and it was frowned upon by our peers if they found this out. We kept it from Coach Hurley because we would probably be kicked off the team or punished. We weren't the ones starting the fights at all but we damn sure would be the ones to finish them.

Matt and Beanie had girlfriends at the time that were cousins. They lived in the downtown section of Jersey City around another crew of guys that we didn't know at all. None of us were from the downtown area. We knew one or two kids from playing ball, but that was it. There was a rumor spread that we didn't like these guys and they didn't like us. Back and forth rumors were being spread and we didn't know where the rumors were coming from at all. This crap with these guys lasted from our freshman year in high school through our senior year.

Fight after Fight after Fight.

The very first fight was with Matt and a kid that liked his girlfriend. This was a crazy day. The kid was a student at St. Mary's High School which was about four blocks from St. Anthony. This happened to be the kid we knew and played basketball with but Matt didn't care. Matt wanted to know what this kid was saying about him and why he wanted to fight. It didn't end well for either one of them, because Matt ended up in handcuffs and the other kid ended up with nonstop blood dripping from his nose. This was a start of a war that we couldn't get out of.

Month after month we would fight. It was getting out of control to the point where these kids would be outside of St. Anthony ready to fight us when we got out of class. They didn't care about coming to the school and being disruptive, they just wanted to fight. We got into a huge fight one day and the beloved Sister Alan came outside and witnessed us in action. We were all outside brawling.

Sister Alan would hear the rumors about us in the schools and how we were with the girls. She was like a mother figure to all of us. She kept us sane and we respected her. She yelled at us and made us come inside. When we got inside she went straight for Marcus. "It's probably because you were messing around with one of those boy's girlfriends," she yelled. We all looked at each other and wanted to laugh but no way were we going to laugh in her face. She told us to get to the gym and we would deal with the situation later.

After practice, we all laughed, teased Marcus, and made jokes about what Sister Alan screamed out. But then we all stopped and thought about it. This fighting was really over the two girls that Matt and Beanie were dating at the time. This all started because of these girls. We didn't know if they were the ones who spread the rumors or if those guys were just jealous, but at the end of the day it was over these girls. The situation was fishy.

We were fresh home from a trip to an AAU Tournament. Matt and I were hanging out downtown with his girlfriend and some of her friends. We sometimes dangled at danger because we knew damn well we were on the enemy's turf, but didn't care. There was something that happened on our trip which made us mad at Beanie and we knew the downtown guys were aiming for Beanie the most. We figured if Beanie decided to pop up and the guys wanted to fight him, we weren't going to help.

We never knew what was on Beanie's mind and sometimes he didn't open up to us much, but Beanie definitely popped up. The word must have spread quickly because out of nowhere about 20 guys came and surrounded us. They weren't there for Matt and me just as we suspected they wouldn't be, they came specifically for Beanie. Beanie and his girlfriend got up to walk off and we followed. We stuck to our ground and weren't going to help as long as he didn't get too hurt in the process.

We knew Beanie could fight so we weren't worried; none of these kids would be able to take him. Only if more than one began to jump on him, but that wasn't a guarantee. We gave him three kids the max, if more than three kids jumped in we would then lend a helping hand. As we were walking to the light rail a kid came out of nowhere and swung a scooter at Beanie's head. In the same motion as the scooter swung, Beanie was dipping back. The scooter just missed his face by an inch.

I lost my mind at that point; I didn't care how mad we were at Beanie. This was my cousin and I loved him too much to sit back and watch any more of the taunting from these assholes. I thought about the time I brought my problem to him in elementary school and he beat the kid up for me. It was time to return the favor!

I stepped into the street where the guys were crowding him, "Fuck that, which one of y'all wants to fight me," as I took my shirt off. One of the kids rushed at me with his hands down and I punched him right in his face. He fell into me spearing me into the car and I flipped him over and started punching him. Beanie squared up with another kid, while Matt squared up with another. Someone tried to sneak up on Beanie and his girlfriend punched the kid. Beanie was beating the breaks off of another guy.

I turned to my right and Matt was tying his sneaker while a kid was punching him in the back. Now I had worn out the kid I was fighting, he was just lying there. I'm looking at Matt and all I could say is, "Matt what the hell are you doing? We are fighting, and you are tying your sneaker while he's punching you!" Matt replied, "Don't worry because as soon as I finish with my sneaker, I'm going to fuck him up." He then turned to the kid and said, "You hear that, I'm going to fuck you up," and when his sneaker was finished being tied it was a wrap from there. Matt hit this kid with the hardest three-piece combination he probably ever got hit with.

Now we all were finished with putting our share of work in and we hear someone scream Matt's name. It was only us three and the girls, and we were all accounted for. Who the hell would be screaming Matt's name? We rushed to the screams and found our cousin Rick in the hallway of a building on the corner getting jumped on. We started beating up on the kids in the hallway while all of their friends were already retreating. As we got them off of Rick, one by one they each started to run.

"Rick, where the hell did you come from?"

We asked him and he explained that he was on the way to come hang out with us when he saw us all fighting and jumped in. We couldn't do nothing but laugh at this point. It was like a scene from a movie or something. We were outnumbered yet still won the battle, and our cousin was forced into a building after he mysteriously popped up and saw us fighting. We couldn't stop laughing at this, we were mad but it was some funny shit.

Our junior year in school Matt happened to be at a party with a crew of guys from the Pocket Snatchers. At this same party were the guys we were going through all the problems with. Matt called me and told me to come help him because they had a few members more. We had gotten to the point that every time we bumped into each other there was a fight. We even tried to leave it alone if we saw them but they would always start the fight by either throwing a bottle or throwing large rocks at us.

Turns out when I showed up that there wasn't just a few more guys. There were a good 60 more guys and this was not a battle we were set to win, but Matt felt like "Hercules" this night or something. Suddenly, a car came speeding down the street. Everyone that was there with Matt started to run and it ended up being only Matt and me on this street with about 60 people from the downtown area. There were so many of them that they looked like an army platoon set to march for war.

The car picked up more speed and I screamed Matt's name out because they were about to try to run him over. I've never really been scared to fight besides the time I was 12, but this night I was scared as shit. I couldn't run and leave my cousin in the street by himself. Matt thinking he was the "Incredible Hulk" almost had us dead or lying in hospital beds because we probably would have been badly beaten.

Matt heard me scream, he turned to me and at the very last second, he jumped back and the car literally swiped his pants. He took off in a full sprint and basically left me because I was in shock that they just tried to run him over. I took flight not too far behind him and the crowd took flight after us.

Not only did the crowd begin to chase us, the car did as well. The car reached the corner before I did and the back door flew open while the car was still in motion. All I saw was a guy in the back seat holding a shotgun and pointing it at me. He yelled out, "Stop running! Stop running!", but there was no way in hell I was stopping. What part of fighting was this? This wasn't how you fought; there was no need for any weapons to fight.

I was scared for my life. If he shot that shotgun I probably would have been shot because you don't need much aim to shoot and hit a target with a shotgun. I darted past everyone that was running losing both of my sneakers. I turned to see if I had time to pick them up but there was no way in the world. As I turned back I ran into someone and fell but I was still in motion and it seemed as if I never fell.

I ended up around the corner where I saw a fence and all I knew was that I was jumping this fence. Everyone else was running in the same direction, but I needed to separate myself. I couldn't see what was over this fence but as soon as I reached the top and was airborne, I was already in motion with no chance of stopping. The homeowner's backyard was full of car parts that were all over the backyard. It was like I jumped straight into a swimming pool of car parts. I was in so much pain but I was alive and no one was chasing me. I walked to the back door and the door was open.

Now I'm in this stranger's home and all I could think about was what if this person is crazy or has a gun. Yet I had nothing to lose, so I took my chances. "Excuse me", I yelled. "Hellooo." No one answered. I repeated myself and a man came downstairs. I raised my hands in the air and apologized for just coming in his house. He then asked, "How did you get in here?" and I replied, "Your back door was open." I explained that these guys had pulled a gun out on me and they were trying to shoot me, but I ran. I asked him if I could use a phone and call for a ride. He was generous and allowed me.

I thought to myself, "Whoever thinks that GOD doesn't exist is a damn fool because once again he saved me!" I was hoping Matt got away safe but there was no way I could know at the moment. My cousin Renard came to pick me up and we went to check on Matt, he was fine. I was done for the night and it was time to go home. This was a crazy night and one I never wished to revisit.

Things were getting out of control. We all stuck by each other and if one fought, we all fought. One of our problems, was all of our problems. We were friends and cousins, but brothers by heart. Matt didn't stick with basketball in high school and senior year tragedy struck. I was home in bed and received a call that Matt had been shot. If I didn't have a game the next day, I probably would have been hanging out with him. Basketball definitely kept us out of trouble at times, and if Matt would have stuck with basketball he would have been home in bed resting for a game just as I was.

I didn't know how badly Matt was hurt or if he even survived. I got one phone call after another, and finally a call from a friend who rode in the ambulance with him. He told me that Matt was fine and the EMS workers said he would be okay. Now this is how secretive we were with not telling our parents. I just found out that my cousin was shot, and once I found out he was okay I just rolled over and went back to sleep. My father told me in the morning that Matt had been shot and I responded by saying I already know. He asked how I knew and why I didn't tell him, I had no answer. We were becoming numb to all the crap that went on in the streets and that wasn't healthy for us.

After visiting Matt in the hospital, he explained the story to me. He was in a pool hall and the guys we were fighting with from downtown were there as well. Matt called me earlier in the night and asked for the gun, but by this time I moved out of Jersey City to Hillside, New Jersey. There was no way I could bring him this gun. Besides, the gun wasn't meant for us to shoot anyone, it was just to scare people off.

I explained this to Matt and he had no intentions to shoot anyone but to scare them so they didn't have to fight, but these were literally street kids. The fighting he wasn't worried about because he could fight. It was just the mere fact that he didn't know what intentions they had. The previous year they pulled a gun on us and he figured they probably had one now. As Matt was leaving, someone fired at him and shot him in his wrist and leg. This was the first time of several times Matt would be shot.

We were all furious and now in war mode. We were only teenagers and we didn't think the right way at all. They had turned to guns because our fighting skills were too good for them. We had a gun but we weren't using it to try and harm anyone or shoot anyone. If it was a fight someone wanted, it was a fight they would get. We didn't need guns because we would fight. Win, lose, or draw, we would fight with no weapons involved. Now these guys wanted to involve guns.

We were in too deep and far ahead of ourselves. We kept this a secret from our parents and we couldn't just tell them because we were scared we would get into trouble. Not only that, we all had a reputation to keep amongst each other. Deep down I know each and every one of us wanted to come forward and say something for our safety but pride was in the way.

We had to be tough, that's how we were raised. If someone told it was a sign of weakness and none of us were weak. I guarantee if one of us told we would have all came together and told as well because we did everything together. We even fought each other, but we all loved each other as brothers and brothers sometimes fight.

We tricked each other into believing that it wasn't right to come forward. At the time, it was foolish and dumb, but we could care less. Somehow, we would escape the danger and end up fine but now they were shooting. We didn't want to start shooting back and although we could, it was not something we were intending to do. We weren't killers nor did we intend to become killers, but if the situation came that we had to take our one little gun and shoot.

We would!

After Matt got shot, we all kind of knew we really needed to calm down and stay away from the streets. It was getting more and more dangerous for us. We were paranoid. Word got around that the downtown crew got into problems with another crew from their area. This was our ticket out of this drama. The focus wasn't on us anymore. We didn't need to be involved in this anyway and eventually it all died down, but we always kept our guards up.

Things weren't always good for us in the streets of Jersey City. The streets made us tough. We fought when we didn't necessarily want to, we turned to violence because we had to, and we carried around an illegal firearm that we shared amongst each other in order to protect ourselves. There were certain things that no one understood. They didn't understand why we were the way we were. Why we always stuck together and didn't want to split up. We bled together, came close to death together, and dealt with all the bullshit there was possible to deal with, together! There was no way in hell our bond was ever going to be broken. We had been through entirely too much. Way too much!

INTERVIEW III

Q: Marcus. In the projects growing up, if the Curries Woods guys were fighting outsiders, did you have an option to fight?
Marcus: *Nah! It ain't no option! Ain't no option! Everything we dealt with back in the day, you know growing up as kids. You fighting! Outsiders fighting the projects, you got to fight!*

Q: Marcus. What happened if you didn't fight?
Marcus: *If you didn't fight you were going to fight when you get back to the projects. It was one or the other! You going to fight one way or the other! But when you fought back in the projects for not fighting, you were fighting to get disciplined. You know. Like you turned your back on your brothers at the end of the day. That's one thing I guess we all brought to our basketball team because we all had the same mentality. If somebody came on your block, Otis's block, Matt's block, y'all have to fight with your block. That's like if somebody came against our team, we had to fight with our team. If you don't fight with your team, it's like what's up! Now you got to fight your team. It's all about loyalty and discipline. Stay true to your family.*

Q: Marcus. How did you feel when I called you and told you I saw your cousin get shot?
Marcus: *I was lost for words when you told me. It was like I thought you were bugging. I'm like whatever, trying to brush it off. Until you know.* **(Paused)** *I could hear it in your voice that you were serious about it. You know, now it's just like you don't know what to expect. It was a little shocking.*

Q: Marcus. Did you have a sense of relief when you found out he was going to be alright?
Marcus: *Yeah, but at first, he was in a coma for a few. Ummm, you know. We didn't know how serious it was. For your family member to be in a coma!*

Not knowing what the situation was, if he was going to make it, or if he was going to die. I was just hurting not knowing if I was going to lose my family member or not.

MISUNDERSTOOD KNUCKLEHEADS

WITHIN OUR FIRST year of being at St. Anthony we built a name for ourselves. This was our very first year that all of us were attending the same school. Most of the time we would meet up at the Boys Club every so often and that was it. Now we would see each other a lot more in school and having basketball workouts after. Shit at this point we spent more time with each other than we spent with family.

When we would meet up at the Boys & Girls Club we would goof off a lot, now we were at St. Anthony and it just gave us more room to goof around and have fun. Usually as a kid going to a new school you are kind of nervous. You won't know anyone but maybe a hand full of kids. The teachers are new, the school setting is new, everything is new. Yet with us, we went to St. Anthony as comfortable as can be.

With all the goofing around and crap we got into, we quickly built a name for ourselves as knuckleheads. We weren't the amazing group of incoming freshmen or labeled as anything good for that matter. We were simply knuckleheads. If you look up the word knucklehead on google you will get a variety of definitions for it.

"Refers to a person of questionable intelligence. The size of the brain being given relative size of a human knuckle. Similar to pinhead."

"Someone of limited intelligence and with a mean nature. Who prefers using their knuckles/fists, to using their head."

"A dunce. A dummy. A very stubborn person or animal."

"A person who doesn't listen, and stays in trouble."

In St. Anthony, the word knucklehead meant Matt, Marcus, Beanie, Otis, Lamar, and Shelton. Together as a group we were all of these definitions summed up in one. When we weren't together the word knucklehead probably wouldn't exist. As teenagers, we didn't look at the bigger picture right away. Life was all about fun and games. We can save the important stuff and the worrying for the adults. Let's just get on this basketball court and get right. To hell with everything else.

Being that Marcus played varsity our freshman year, he was kind of able to separate himself from us. The things that we would get into, Marcus wasn't around because he was already playing for Coach Hurley. Things were different when you played varsity ball. Varsity rules weren't the same as the junior varsity or freshman rules. We had a lot more time to goof around but the varsity team was constantly busy.

In addition to goofing around and having fun, the drama with the downtown crew had escalated. It honestly kind of changed us all. We already grew up in environments where it was either play sports or get taken in by the streets. Survive, go to jail, or end up dead. Those were our options. It was very easy to get caught up in anything in the areas of Jersey City that we lived in. There were drugs all around, and you could easily pick your poison. Marijuana, cocaine, or heroin, whichever drug you wanted you could have access to it. Every other block had its own private pharmacy. You could buy the drugs to use or you could buy the drugs to sell. Not only drugs, but alcohol was also readily available at a very young age.

Doesn't seem like something young kids would have a chance to take interest in, but some kids we grew up with were raised into the life. Shit, born into the life. In elementary school, I was in the third or fourth-grade and I had a very close friend. We met each other in kindergarten and as we went up in grades we were in the same classes. He came to school looking very sad one day and wasn't looking like his normal self. I asked him what was wrong and he told me that he wouldn't be coming to school anymore. He then broke down and started crying.

I wrapped my arm around his shoulder. "It's all good man, we'll still be cool, no worries. You are probably going to attend Public School #15 now, right?" He gathered himself together and responded, "No it's not like that, my mother sold me to this white guy for drugs! She's a drug addict. I don't know what's going to happen and she told me not to say anything but promised everything would be alright."

At this very young age I knew exactly what he just told me and I couldn't bring myself to believe that what he said was true. It couldn't be true. I comforted him and told him that there was no way that was going to happen, then I kind of brushed it off. Yet, within a few days I didn't see him anymore. Which then raised a red flag in my head and I started to wonder where he was. I still didn't believe that his mother would do such a thing, it was impossible.

One day after school, as I was leaving I noticed his mother standing in the spot outside the gate that she would always pick him up at. When I saw this I said to myself, "See I knew he was going to come back to school." Maybe I just hadn't seen him or he was now in a different class, but he never came out of the building. As I'm standing there waiting for him to run out of the school doors and go to his mom, I glance over to his mom and she is crying. She is standing at the gate just crying. I knew something was wrong and my friend asked me not to tell because him and his mom would get into trouble if anyone found out.

As the days went by I hoped and prayed that he would pop up and come to school, yet every day he didn't show. Every day his mother was still outside at her spot looking as if he was coming out, and every day that she came I stayed and I watched. After a while she stopped coming and I would see her in the neighborhood looking very strung out on drugs. Eventually I never saw her again and I never saw him again either.

I never told because I promised him I wouldn't, but I should have told. I didn't want him to be in trouble and he loved his mom so I didn't want her to be in trouble either. Still today I think about him and just hope that he turned out okay, shit I just hope that he is alive at least. I was a kid and I didn't understand the severity of the situation. I didn't think that his mom actually sold him until I got older and I started to think that his mother came every day to that same spot at the fence and she cried. Maybe she did really sell him, but I never found out what actually happened.

I realized how powerful drugs were at the time and I never wanted to get involved with any kind of hard drugs that could make a person lose themselves. I saw how the people on drugs in my area looked, they were like zombies. The drug dealers didn't care what age you were, whose mother, father, brother, or sister you were. If you wanted the drugs, they sold them to you. At a very young age I watched my friend's mother break down from drugs, I was almost lured into a car, I was shot at, seen guys chasing another guy shooting at him, a girl I went to school with turn into a drug addict in the eighth grade, and so on. All of this took place in just elementary school when going to St. Anthony High School wasn't even a thought in my mind yet.

We all grew up in very similar environments like this and basketball was our key to survival. Basketball was our way out and if it didn't separate us from the streets in some way, our lives would be very different now. We all bonded and stuck together. So when we obtained the knucklehead name in school from Coach Hurley and others, we kind of didn't pay any mind to it. Yeah, there were things that we did that we shouldn't have done, but what kid or teenager is perfect? No one understood the things we went through and it was because we didn't tell anyone either. We kept everything to ourselves and just stuck together.

When we all started playing for Coach Hurley, it kept us out of the streets to a certain extent. We still had to go home after practices and we still had to live in our areas. If one of us had a problem, we all had a problem. That was just the way it went, we had to protect each other. Therefore, when Coach tried to separate us so that we could not be that group of knuckleheads, it was impossible.

It seemed like at all times if it wasn't one thing it was another. There was never a time when we could just be focused on basketball and school ever. We were into clothes, girls, and having fun. With nice clothes brought girls to you and also led attention to you by whatever stick up kids were in town. There was book smart and street smart. Yeah, book smart you needed and our parents instilled that in us. Street smart was something we had to learn on our own. You could learn it the easy way or the hard way. Either way you needed to be street smart to survive.

For me, I learned at a very early age after almost being kidnapped, robbed, and shot at. After these things happened, life was never really the same for me. I constantly watched my back. I started paying attention to my surroundings a lot more. If a car was on my street that I didn't notice, I avoided being near it. If someone looked funny, I avoided them. Gun shots would sporadically ring out at night around the same time the 10 o'clock commercial came on which said, "It's 10 o'clock, do you know where your children are?" My answer was always, "Yes, in my future wife's stomach." Boy oh boy how corny was that.

As kids, we were all on edge and moved around cautiously. We had to be tough, street smart, and that knucklehead definition that stated, "Someone of limited intelligence and with a mean nature. Who prefers using their knuckles/fists, to using their head." Of course, minus the limited intelligence part. The streets made us mean and at points it seemed there was always someone out to get you. Instead of being the person to be the victim, if we sensed someone trying to harm one of us, we used our knuckles to protect ourselves.

We felt our knucklehead name was given to us because we were misunderstood. It was very easy to look at us and hear the things that we did and say those guys just don't get it. We got it, we just had so much shit on our minds that it distracted us and the only time we could goof around was when we were in environments that we felt safe. So when we got into trouble in school for goofing around, it was merely because in the streets there was no such thing as goofing around. It was life or death. We hung out with each other outside of school but we had to constantly watch our surroundings. This took away from the fun. Shit, it took away from us actually being normal teenagers.

St. Anthony was our safe zone. We could come to school, be comfortable, and worry free. There were plenty of teenagers in that school that would have never lasted in any public school in town. This was a well-known school for basketball, but for those that didn't play ball, this school was a necessity for them. The other Catholic schools were too pricey and the public schools were too risky.

We played on basketball courts throughout the city, in city tournaments and just pick up games. Some of the tournaments weren't made up of kids that played on teams in high school or so on. There were kids that played in these tournaments that were high school age, but didn't go to school because they were on the streets. Sometimes older guys played who didn't even have respect for the game and just wanted to be bullies on the court.

When it came to basketball or a challenge, we didn't back down. You could be a gangster all you wanted, but on the basketball court you had better bring your A-game. So sometimes playing basketball on the streets entailed for you to have an exit plan just in case shit got real. I remember playing at a Bayside Park league against a team full of members from the bloods gang. My coach at the time, Allen Brooks, got in my head before the game.

"Oh Shelton, you haven't dunked on anybody all season. You're out here all the time dunking when no one is around, but in the game you never dunk."

He got me motivated and I told him that I would not take a layup or jump shot the entire game. I told him that every shot attempt would be a dunk attempt. Sure enough, every shot I took was an attempted dunk, but one dunk almost caused a problem. I was coming down the left side of the court on a fast break and my opponent was coming down the right side at a fast speed. As I sized him up, I could see the rim, and I knew he would go for the block. I angled my body with the left side facing the rim and leaped into the air with my guide hand up. He jumped for the block and with my guide hand in the way I used it to distance him from reaching the block attempt.

BOOM!!!

Dunked on! Foul, and-one!

The entire park went crazy. The refs had to pause the game because everyone was on the court. The guy then comes up to me and says, "A yo, don't do that shit no more for real or we are fighting," and I responded by saying, "Don't jump no more. You jump again, you are getting dunked on again." If I had backed down I would have looked like a punk and when someone has the slightest feeling that they can take advantage of you, they go for the jugular. A basketball game was on the verge of becoming a brawl or maybe a shooting because I dunked on this guy and he was embarrassed.

My team ended up winning the game and I was sure we were going to fight because I didn't stop dunking the ball. If I would have let the threat bother me, my game would have changed because I would have been worried. Fighting had become a norm for me. Hearing gun shots and seeing guns were a norm for me. I became numb to it. A situation like this was why I strongly felt I needed a gun. I was scared of what could happen, so I felt having a gun would definitely make things better.

I stated before everyone had access to the gun and we took it everywhere. Not only did I feel safe, the guys felt safe. All the nervousness was out the picture and we were protected. I gave Lamar the gun one day to walk to his girlfriend's house and things went south somehow. He called me to tell me that his girl called his stepfather and told him he had a gun. We met at a friend's house and I took the gun so that I can put it away at my girlfriend's house at the time. As I went back to our friend's house and we began to leave, Lamar took off and ran as he screamed, "Yo that's my step pops!"

This car was all the way down the street and it blew my mind how he even saw that far to know it was his stepfather. Sure enough, it was his stepfather pulling up and he pulled over.

"Where's Lamar at?" We quickly responded saying we didn't know.

"Who has the gun? I know y'all have a gun, who has it?" We looked and said, "We don't have no gun," with the dumbest looks on our faces.

"Oh, you guys think you know about the streets huh? You don't know shit about these streets! These streets will eat you up! Y'all really think y'all know about the streets! All these gangsters out here will kill you! Tell Lamar I'm looking for him and he can run, but can't hide!"

Now instead of being nervous of being robbed or having a gun pulled out on me, I was nervous that Lamar's stepfather was going to tell my father we had a gun. I asked Lamar why he even let his girlfriend see the gun and he said she was searching in his stuff while he was sleep. So if my father asked me, I would have to stick with a lie and say I don't know what's going on. I knew if his stepfather told my father he would question me and maybe start searching to see if I had the gun so I left it at my girlfriend's house.

A few weeks later, I was hanging out at my girl's house and Matt called me stating that there was a car full of guys staged around the corner and they looked very suspicious to him. He wanted me to bring the gun just in case, but I didn't have it. I had literally just given the gun to another friend who felt he needed it to walk home. As I'm calling him for the gun, I walked to Matt to see if I saw the car and if I could get a description of the guys at least.

While waiting on our friend, the car pulls off from the corner that it was on. We are now watching as we stand behind this big metal box shaped item on the sidewalk, which may have had electrical wiring in it or something. The car picked up speed and gunshots rang out. We ducked behind the metal object and the car took off.

Matt strongly felt it was guys from the downtown crew because we had just been fighting with them not too long ago. Things were out of control and could only get worse. I felt I would end up in jail or dead because I was getting caught up in the streets. "Live by the gun, die by the gun." It was literally turning into that and the streets were becoming more and more dangerous as we were getting older.

I began to wonder if we had become the same guys that we were trying to protect ourselves from. We were basketball players. Our parents raised us right and we were doing all the wrong things possible. We had to change or things wouldn't end well for us. The more and more I tried to focus on basketball, the worse things seemed to get outside the basketball courts. This environment we were living in had taken its toll on us.

We all felt we needed to walk home with a gun to feel safe. Which meant that every time we stepped outside we had an illegal firearm on us. We weren't out robbing people or doing anything of that nature, but we were in fact breaking the law. The streets pulled us down and out of fear we rather had broken the law instead of walking the straight path. The streets were no good for us. Eventually the gun ended up in the possession of police officers before anything tragic could happen. By that time, we would all have four years to be away from our environment as we all went to college.

Our parents raised us the best way they could and I would say they all did great jobs. With all the nonsense going on around our areas, they knew we needed to stick together. It was all a part of being able to survive where we came from. Alone we could hold our grounds if we had to, but together we were stronger. If it made us safe being together, it's what needed to be done. Our parents taught us right from wrong, that education was important, and how to survive.

When my parents moved me to Hillside, New Jersey it was a better environment for me and I didn't have to be in Jersey City as much. I could rest easy and I didn't have that fear of anyone running up on me or shooting at me. I didn't hear gunshots every week that woke me up from my sleep. Still I stayed alert everywhere I went, it was impossible for me to shake off the tightness I had from growing up in Jersey City. I was changed. In some way, I was a knucklehead. We all were and we were forced to be. We did whatever it took to survive. For us it was basketball, our parents, Coach Hurley, and being misunderstood knuckleheads!

INTERVIEW IV

Q: What did you guys think about being considered knuckleheads?

Beanie: *I don't think we were knuckleheads. It's just that, coming from where we came from, it was just like we did things differently. We thought differently. So coming from somebody on the outside looking in, they don't know what we are really thinking. They don't know what's going on in our heads. What type of situations we are dealing with when we got to travel to school or when we leave school. When we go to practice or when we leave practice. Nobody understood what was going on in our lives outside of St. Anthony. So I wouldn't consider us knuckleheads. We were just trying to survive, that's all. Coming from where we come from.*

Marcus: *To be honest we were knuckleheads. I ain't even going to lie about it. We did what we wanted because we didn't like what was being said about us. So we continued to do the opposite of what people wanted from us. We also wanted to do the right things as well. Knuckleheads! Yeah, we were knuckleheads.* **(Paused)** *But look at it like this right! When they considered us knuckleheads, we still had to keep the street mentality in us. So when we left from being down there with the, "Proper people," to go back to the hood, we were considered normal motherfuckers! Like we weren't considered knuckleheads. That was just the way we had to be growing up in Jersey City! It ain't being a knucklehead. Knucklehead to them was looking tough and not taking shit from nobody. That was being a knucklehead. But that's how you had to be on the streets of Jersey City. You have to have the mentality like whatever! You going to do what you have to do to get by.*

Otis: *I liked being called knuckleheads! I liked everything about it! I just used that as motivation. I liked everything that Coach Hurley said as far as trying to discipline us. Telling us that we are not going to win, or him saying we weren't as good as other teams. I know the way he said things sometimes might come off messed up, but I just used it as motivation. I didn't take it for how he said it, I took what he said and that made me get back to myself. I used to be the one to quit, like who are you talking to like that! You know what, Nah I don't need this. You know what I'm* *saying?* **(Laughing)** *But I knew that I didn't have discipline ever! My mom's ain't going to discipline me! No other coaches were yelling at me! So I think I needed that part of it and it was great for me. I got so many memories of it that I can sit here and talk for days about it.*

PLAYING FOR COACH BOB HURLEY

I HAVE TO admit, we were all told that we needed tough skin to play for Coach Hurley and that he had a shit full of rules. Somehow, we all figured that nothing could break us and we would all be fine. In the end, it showed how tough we really were because not all of us lasted. Even though a majority of us did make it all four years, we still left with shattered dreams.

We went into the school originally as a crew of six without Lamar Alston who ended up going to Marist High School his freshman year and later transferring to St. Anthony High School his sophomore year. We were down Milly from the start and Matt didn't even make it to play for the varsity team. So by our junior year when we all officially played for the varsity team, there were only five of us out of the seven. Marcus, Beanie, Otis, Lamar, and me.

It was our junior year that we realized that this thing could end up anyway and that meant good or bad. However, we didn't know what was going to happen or which one of us would end up screwing up next. It wasn't like we intentionally made mistakes, because our intentions coming into the school was very different than what we displayed. There were plenty of other things on our minds which tarnished our focus and Coach Hurley wasn't just any coach doing this to receive a check. He lived basketball, he took the sport seriously.

Every day that you showed up to practice you had better bring your all. Any game that you showed up to there had better not be a charge or loose ball that you missed because on the bench you would go. Any problem that you had outside of the gym had better been left outside the door before you walked into practice or a game. This was very easily said, but no way in the world was it an easy task to have done.

Coach Hurley would immediately pick up on any player slouching and he would ride you until you performed to his standards. If you didn't perform to his standards the door wasn't too far. You could get kicked out of practice faster than the drop of a dime.

"Guess what, it's Valentine's Day and already you guys are sitting in my gym playing like a bunch of soft asses, just going through all of the motions!"

Coach Hurley seemed to say this to us every Valentine's Day and it still sticks in my head today, because following that statement we would all get kicked right out of the gym within 30 minutes into practice.

"That's it, take your "Ruddy Pooh," "Candy Asses," across the street to the mall and spend time with your little girlfriends. Go to the movies, buy them flowers and gifts, because you all are probably better at that than you are at basketball."

The mind games, the scare tactics, and the instilled fear we had in us all from Coach Hurley. He knew what he was doing and he did it well. Not only did he do it well, he was by far the best damn high school coach in the nation.

At times, we didn't understand him at all but we knew what he said meant something. We came into St Anthony as a team thinking we were hot shit and unstoppable. Marcus was the only one of us that started off playing varsity ball as a freshman. We quickly found out how much we weren't as good as we thought. If we went to any average school we would all have probably taken over the school and started varsity for all four years, but St. Anthony was a basketball powerhouse. We heard about the very high expectations of Coach Hurley and that he was a firm coach. Yet we figured, come on, how firm could he be?

I knew Coach Hurley coming up as a kid. He was a good friend to the family and even put a good word in for my father to get his job as a Probation Officer. This was a kind man and I didn't understand all the fuss about how he was such a firm coach and strict. He didn't seem that way to me and I knew him for years. Well I guess knowing him as a kid was completely different than knowing him as a basketball player on his team. When it came to basketball, Coach Hurley was strictly about his business, all work and no play.

We quickly began to understand what everyone meant when they said you must have tough skin playing for Coach Hurley. This definitely wasn't an easy task. If you're not tough enough he will break you and it will drive you to the point of hating the sport altogether. It will drive you to the point that it would seem as though you never loved playing basketball at all.

In my opinion, every one of us touched our breaking point at one time or another, everyone except for Marcus. Coach Hurley wasn't the type of coach you could give a response to or explain your reasoning for doing what you did. No, it was his way or the highway. You weren't going to contradict his way of running his basketball program. He built the program and he knew it best, so it was shut up and listen when it came to this St. Anthony team.

Sophomore year as we moved up to play for the varsity team, we were granted the opportunity of being a part of the State Champions and Tournament of Champions team led by Dwayne Lee, Donald Copeland, and Elijah Ingram. Coach Hurley was sure to let us know that we didn't contribute a drip of sweat to these achievements. Yeah, we might have played in what some would call sloppy seconds, but if those guys didn't build a large enough lead we wouldn't have stepped foot on the court.

Right then and there is when the mind games began. I called them his motivational tactics. What he said was 100 % true. We knew this, but it was something about being able to experience that feeling that gave us the drive to want to do it on our own and never hear those words leave his mouth again. Still, every so often Coach Hurley would take that finger of his and point up to the wall.

"You see that banner up there; you guys didn't contribute shit to the past years of State Champions and Tournament of Champions and you come to practice just going through the motions!"

This stemming from a missed layup, a lazy effort to go after a loose ball, or maybe even not taking a charge in practice. There wasn't a moment that he wasn't on our backs about something. In his eyes, we were knuckleheads. Now if he really felt that way about us is still unclear to me, but I'll be damned if it didn't constantly roll off his tongue.

At times, it felt like Coach Hurley was trying to split us up. Like he didn't want us bonding the way we were. I guess to him when we were together we didn't challenge each other enough to be better players. Our friendships were so strong that we didn't like to embarrass one another on the court because we didn't want to hear Coach Hurley screaming on anyone out of the crew. I must admit we were relaxed when it came to challenging each other in practice. If it were against other players we tried to kick their ass, but against each other we were laid back.

We could never figure Coach Hurley out. No matter how much we studied him and tried to, we could just never figure out what pleased him. Beanie once asked, "How can you please someone that cannot be pleased?" This question stumped us all because it seemed as if he was never happy with us. Occasionally he would compliment us but it was very rare. We were so used to the word knucklehead that when he said it we all turned and at times it wasn't even one of us he was talking to.

Every so often Coach Hurley would go on a kick out rampage and some of us would get kicked out of practice. It went from one of us, to all five of us, but you never knew who it would be. "The Kick Out Stories," that's what we call them, because every so often we hang out and reminisce about being kicked out of practice all the time. Valentine's Day was the best. We just knew we would be kicked out, and by the second time we figured Coach Hurley just needed a reason to go home and spend the day with Mrs. Hurley.

One Saturday we had a practice at St. Peters College and fresh into practice Lamar was screwing up. Within 15 minutes Coach Hurley stopped practice. "Lamar what the hell are you doing? We have been running drills for the past 15 minutes and you haven't even broken a sweat! You know what, go home!" As he walked away and took a glimpse at me, "Shelton you go home too, that's your boy right! GET OUT!" I was confused, what the hell just happened I asked myself. I had been kicked out of the gym for what I thought was nothing.

When we got dressed and arrived at the bus stop, not too far behind us was our teammate Justin Lewis. Before we could even say anything, Justin opened his mouth, "He kicked me out too and don't ask why because I don't know," all we could do was laugh. It wasn't worth a damn to say but Coach, what did I do, because you would be embarrassed if you did that. Therefore, we would just take our free day off. GOD knows we didn't get many of them anyway.

He was a loose cannon and you never knew what the hell would happen. The most memorable Kick Out Story had nothing to do with our crew at all. In fact, it didn't even have anything to do with any of the players on his team. After this one, we all thought Coach Hurley was a straight up maniac! He loved basketball to death because this day he kicked his own wife out of the gym. Yes, he kicked Mrs. Hurley out of the gym. Not only did he kick her out of the gym, but it was snowing outside. It was not like little flurry snowflakes falling. It was bad outside, I mean winter snow storm and knee-high snow bad.

We were in the beginning stage of practice and Mrs. Hurley walked into the gym. We all gladly said hello, we loved Mrs. Hurley. She was the best. As practice continued, Mrs. Hurley was still around and we could hear her as she kept talking to Coach, but it wasn't bothering us one bit.

The next thing you know Coach Hurley turned to Mrs. Hurley and said, "Honey I'm running practice here, go home." The looks on our faces were priceless. This man just kicked his wife out of the gym. We knew for sure he would be sleeping on the couch when he got home.

The moment practice was over we rushed into the locker room. Beanie started it up.

"Yoooooo, did he really kick Mrs. Hurley out in the middle of the snow storm! Yo he is fucking crazy for real. If he kicked his own wife out of the gym, he would kick anyone out the gym!"

I doubt Beanie was wrong about what he said and all I could say was, "Well at least he didn't kick her out the way he kicks us out. At least he said Honey first. He at least buttered her up a little."

We all just sat in the locker room and laughed about it. That was the most insane thing we could ever think of a coach doing.

When Coach Hurley kicked his wife out of practice that day, it really made me realize how much this man took this sport to heart. This wasn't a hobby or just something to do. He loves the game of basketball. If basketball were a woman, he would be married to her because he and basketball are inseparable.

When we walked around with our St. Anthony's gear on, people would always say, "Wow, you play for Coach Hurley? You must be good." What they didn't understand was that you didn't need to be good to play for Coach Hurley. You needed work ethic and dedication and he would give you a chance. Coach Hurley could mold the worse player into one of the best. It makes me think of Ahmad Nivins. When Ahmad came to St. Anthony High School his basketball coordination had not been fully developed, but that would soon change. Ahmad wanted to learn, Ahmad wanted to get better, and Coach Hurley coached.

Ahmad didn't have great post moves or perfect footwork on the court, but Coach Hurley had his way of making sure you learned what you needed to learn. Whether he spent extra time doing big man drills in practice, or in the off-season making sure you were at camps and playing AAU ball somewhere. If he saw you had the work ethic and the potential, he would teach you. Ahmad had the work ethic, that's exactly why it landed him a scholarship to St. Josephs College and eventually getting drafted 2nd round in the 2009 NBA draft.

Playing for Coach Hurley wasn't like playing for any other coach. He ran a tight ship and if you didn't obey the rules you were fired. We all were dealing with outside issues and we couldn't talk to Coach Hurley about these issues. I can't really say we couldn't talk to him about our issues we had going on, but it's more of the fact that we didn't feel comfortable talking to him about things. I'm quite sure he would have listened; however, the actions he may have taken is what we were really unprepared for. Knowing the actions that he may have taken was the reason we never approached him to talk about our problems.

Coach Hurley was a hands-on coach, and when I say hands-on I mean on the court with us. If a player screwed up he would pause practice and tell you to step aside as he took your position on the court. He knew every single position and every spot on the court you were supposed to be at for every play. If you didn't cut hard enough to the basket, he would step in and show you how hard you were supposed to make that basket cut. If he didn't like the way you boxed out for a rebound, he would step in and show you how to box out. How to make sure the player never got around you or over you without getting an over the back call. Play after play, drill after drill, Coach Hurley would be on your ass. On your ass from the moment you stepped foot into the gym, in fact from before you stepped into the gym.

School was fresh out and of course Marcus, Beanie, Otis, Lamar, and I were all outside of the school flirting with girls and goofing around. Knowing that practice was starting in about 20 minutes, it seemed as if Coach Hurley just appeared out of the wind.

"Here it is 20 minutes before practice is about to start, and you group of knuckleheads are sitting here bullshitting around. You would think that 20 minutes before practice you guys would be in the gym dressed already and warming up, working on your games. I'll tell you what! I'm going to walk this way and you go that way! If I get to that gym before you guys, we will have practice without touching a ball!"

We all looked at each other with the 'oh shit face.' We began walking in the direction he told us to walk. Knowing that he gave us the longer distance to get to the gym out of the two separate ways it took to get there from the school. As soon as we hit the corner out of his sight we took off in full sprints, laughing as we ran. We knew either way if we got there first or not, we had already pissed him off.

Yet, he was absolutely right and sometimes we needed that extra push just to get our shit together. We got to the gym before he did but he still walked in only a split second after we entered the gym. We were all mind blown because we knew damn well we just ran to the gym. There was no way he could get there at almost the exact same time. So it was either he walked fast as hell or he ran. Either way we knew we had better have a good practice or it would be a hard practice.

I don't think that any of us could say it was easy playing under Coach Hurley's supervision. It was definitely a roller coaster. Every day that I went to practice I was nervous until I stepped foot on that basketball court. Sometimes the nervousness came from something that was said the day before or from the fact that I wanted to do so well. I didn't want to go into practice and screw up. I'm quite sure everyone felt that way, but I can say I definitely had those feelings.

It seemed like Coach Hurley would like to stir things up to make us compete with each other and to practice harder. We all played for several other coaches at some point in our lives and as usual some coaches have their favorites. They may favor the best player, the hustle player, the shooter, the big man, or maybe even that one player that just loves to take a charge no matter what. Coach Hurley was not like that. Yes, he liked all of those things, but favoritism was not a word found in his vocabulary. If he had a choice, he would remove it from the dictionary because it didn't belong. You have to work for your respect on the court, good player or not.

With Coach Hurley, things were tough enough to handle just coming from him. So when other coaches and teachers tried to emulate his ways it made things even more difficult. The coaching staff fed off of Coach Hurley. If he said the sky was pink, they had better damn well say the sky sure is pink today coach. For this reason, we called the entire coaching staff "The Yes Men." If Coach Hurley came down on us and turned to the coaching staff and said right guys, everyone's response would be, "Right Coach." Maybe one of them wasn't even paying attention because they saw something else and he had no idea what the hell he was agreeing to at the time. However, his answer was, "Right Coach."

That part became annoying and I do have to be honest, of all the coaches, occasionally Coach Ben Gamble would pull you to the side and enlighten you on what's going on. Yet, he as well was in that boat with The Yes Men. Coach Gamble was the assistant coach directly behind Coach Hurley and I respected him a lot. He disappointed me as a role model the summer going into my junior year in high school. As a coach and a man that I looked up to, he really disappointed me and it discouraged me.

We played in a summer league at Seton Hall University and it was a very close game. If I can recall, we were up one point against our opponents. Thomas Hall, one of the guards at the time, was guarding a good shooter from the opposing team and Coach Hurley told everyone to stick with their man. Coach Hurley was into the game watching what he was watching, Coach Gamble saw something different. Coach Gamble screamed out, "Thomas, go and trap! Go and trap!" As Thomas goes to trap, the ball gets swung to Thomas's man and he nails a three-pointer, all net.

At this point, Thomas has the 'what the fuck' face on because no one rotated to pick up the shooter, and no one rotated because Coach Hurley just told everyone to stick to their man. For some reason, Coach Hurley didn't hear Coach Gamble yell to Thomas to go and trap. Coach Hurley's hands go up into a T-shaped form as he yells for a timeout.

"TIME OUT REFEREE! TIME OUT!"

The players run to the bench, Thomas had a look of disgust on his face because no one rotated. Thomas didn't have the slightest idea that he was about to be screamed at because he was informed right out of the prior huddle to stick to his man. He knew exactly what he was told, and he also knew exactly what he heard being yelled from the bench.

As a player, when you hear any coach yelling from the bench, you do what that coach tells you to do. Coach Hurley might not have yelled it at the time, but you assume he said something to the coaching staff for them to yell out, go and trap. Thomas gets to the bench and Coach Hurley goes off.

"WHAT THE FUCK WERE YOU THINKING?"

"WHAT DID I JUST TELL EVERYONE TO DO BEFORE YOU LEFT THE HUDDLE?"

Thomas replies, "Stay with your man."

"STAY WITH YOUR MAN!"

"STAY WITH YOUR MAN!"

"SO WHY THE HELL DID YOU GO AND TRAP?"

"WHO TOLD YOU TO GO AND TRAP?"

"WHO TOLD YOU TO GO AND TRAP?"

Thomas attempts to reply looking at Coach Gamble to step in and answer the question. Thomas knew and we all knew that even though Coach Hurley was asking that question, there was no answer that would come out of his mouth that Coach Hurley would accept. He might not even get the answer all the way out before Coach Hurley would cut him off. As he attempts to respond, sure enough Coach Hurley started back up.

"This is why you are not going to be playing as much as you feel you deserve to be on the court! Derrick Mercer, a sophomore, will be this team's point guard!"

"HOW STUPID CAN YOU BE?"

"HOW STUPID?"

"Your man who is the best shooter on the team was left wide open! You decided to go and trap and now we are down! Sit your ass on the bench where you belong and get used to it!"

His voice traveled through the entire gym, everyone watching. Everyone! Thomas had a look of embarrassment on his face, he was hurt. We couldn't stand up and tell Coach Hurley that Coach Gamble clearly yelled to Thomas to go and trap. The only person that might get away with informing Coach Hurley of Thomas's decision to go and trap was Coach Gamble himself.

Coach Gamble watched as Thomas was screamed on. He stood there and watched. He didn't attempt to step in and say Coach I made a mistake. I told him to go and trap. There was not a word or a peep out of him during Coach Hurley yelling at the top of his lungs. He didn't even have eye contact. It was at that point I began to become disheartened when it came to Coach Gamble.

It was hard enough as a player to play for Coach Hurley alone, without support from the assistant coaches and the rest of the coaching staff it was even harder. At times, we needed some encouragement and a push here or there to get us through. We didn't need things like that. I never asked Thomas if Coach Gamble even came to him personally and apologized or what the situation was, but it was wrong. The respect level went down the drain from there.

When you were in the "doghouse" which meant you were on Coach Hurley's bad side, it was sometimes hard to get out. You had to bust your ass to get out of the doghouse and once you got out, you had to bust your ass not to be put back in. Never a dull moment at all.

Coach Hurley was very unpredictable, very unpredictable. You could be thrown in the doghouse for the simplest thing; something that you thought was so stupid. If he wanted it done, it needed to be done. For instance, taking a charge. Taking a charge was important to him. In a game understood, but he needed it done in practice as well. After all, practice makes perfect, right?

If you missed a charge in practice, we could end up doing charging drills for 30 minutes. My train of thought was, why risk getting hurt in practice by taking charges? On top of the fact I valued my family jewels. Yet, practice makes perfect and I didn't like to practice charges. I found myself in a summer league game missing a perfect charge in a tight game.

Again, at Seton Hall University in a summer league game. Tie score and the player is driving down the middle out of control. I didn't take the charge and all hell broke loose.

Coach Hurley calls for a time out.

"WHY DIDN'T YOU TAKE THAT CHARGE?"

"HE'S DRIVING OUT OF CONTROL DOWN THE MIDDLE OF THE LANE!"

"WHY DIDN'T YOU STEP UP, SET YOUR FEET, AND TAKE THE DAMN CHARGE!"

"SIT YOUR ASS!"

"WHAT WOULD BE OUR BALL WITH A CHANCE TO TAKE A TWO POINT LEAD IS NOW US DOWN TWO!"

In the doghouse I went. I quickly realized how important it was to take that charge in practice. If you practice it, it becomes natural and you won't second guess yourself in the game situation. Needless to say, Coach was right, taking charges in practice wasn't stupid at all.

There were some things that Coach Hurley would do that were just so hilarious at times and we knew damn well not to let him catch us laughing. As hard as it was to keep a straight face, we figured out a way.

We were running drills at the beginning of practice and Coach Hurley was standing in the middle of the court. He was walking back and forth with his whistle in his mouth watching and coaching as we ran the drills. Beanie ran into him accidentally and said, "Sorry Coach, are you alright?" Well why did Beanie ask that?

He blew the whistle, and everyone came to a pause.

"Ahmad just ran into me and had the nerve to ask if I was alright. Ahmad are you serious? If you punched me with all of your strength, you wouldn't hurt me! If I gave you a bat and you took your best swing and hit me with the bat, you wouldn't hurt me! That's how soft you are!"

We didn't know where this came from, but it was funny as shit. I took my jersey and wiped the sweat off my face several times, just so I could hide from laughing. You never knew what you would get out of Coach on any given day. You never knew what you did on or off the court to piss him off.

Marcus, Lamar, and Otis were the only ones on our team that were 18 years old our senior year and we had a terrible practice one day. Of course, we pissed him off and he felt some kind of way. It was merely the end of practice and he stops practice.

"How many of you guys here are 18 or older?"

Marcus, Otis, and Lamar raised their hands.

"Do you guys want a piece of me? Any one of you that wants a piece of me for any reason, one by one we can go into the locker room. I guarantee you that I would be the one walking out without any marks or bruising. I would roll my sleeves up, get in my stance, and punch you out one by one! You guys are a bunch of soft asses! Here we are in your senior years and you come to practice and go through the motions! You half ass practice and have attitudes like your hot shit. No one here has scholarships lined up!

NO ONE!"

After he finally stopped yelling and we all got into the locker room I couldn't help but taunt the three of them.

"If it was me and he offered me into the locker room I would have said let's go. Y'all are all punks."

Everyone began to laugh and talk shit because we knew he wasn't serious and we knew damn well I wouldn't have said let's go, but it was more to what he said. It was our senior year and none of us had any idea as to what colleges we were going to. Here we are the number two team in the nation, number one team in New Jersey, and none of us had the slightest idea if any schools were even interested in one of us.

We had so much shit going with us that Coach Hurley constantly reminded us how he had no choice but to inform college coaches what kind of kids we were. He didn't want to mislead these coaches and have them thinking they were getting angels if they offered anyone of us scholarships. He had to be honest, his name was on the line and I understood that later. These coaches wouldn't be getting your average teenagers. Marcus and Lamar were already fathers. Deep down all we were was a bunch of kids from the hood that could put a basketball in the rim.

When everyone asks how it was playing for Coach Hurley, the answer varies and it's not simple at all.

Outstanding, Amazing, Awesome, Best Experience Ever, Life Changing, Motivating, Spontaneous, and then you have to add, STRESSFUL!

Great experience all around, but very stressful!

When you are playing for what you consider the greatest high school coach in the world, you are excited and want to learn. However, instead of it being just that, it comes with much more. It comes with what some would call verbal abuse, mind games, extreme disciplinary tactics, and child labor. Not literally, but from your young teenage years until you graduate St. Anthony High School, basketball is no longer a sport. It becomes your full-time job with zero tolerance. Zero tolerance for lateness, sick days, call outs, excuses, and so on.

I began to lose love for the sport, it was no longer fun after a while. I was scared to make a mistake, to cause a turnover, miss a jump shot, a layup, a charge, or anything of that sort. It came to the point I couldn't play basketball how I knew to play it. Instead I played in fear. I wanted to play this sport I loved so much growing up as a kid, but it became a job more than a sport. I found myself not putting all my effort into playing anymore, not caring, not even wanting to be in the gym.

Playing for other coaches such as Derreck Mercer Sr., Ike Ford, Frank Burno, Joseph Whalen, Anthony DiGiovanni, Carlos Cueto, Joseph Clinton, and so on, was much easier than stepping on a court with Coach Hurley as your coach. These coaches you could talk to, these coaches you had room for error, these coaches were 100 times more laid back than Coach Hurley. One can misunderstand what I am saying when I make these statements, don't get me wrong if you made a mistake any of these coaches would still get in your ass. Yet, they didn't demand that same perfection out of you that Coach Hurley did. If you missed a shot but came down and got a steal leading your team to score, these coaches forgot about that missed shot. Good defense, way to go.

Coach Hurley could care less about that steal you got that led to your team scoring. What about the missed shot before the steal? That was still on his mind. What about that charge you missed the play before, the loose ball you didn't go after, the free throws you missed? "Sit your ass," and right to the bench you go.

It was like night and day playing for Coach Hurley. Never knew if it would be sunny, rainy, cold, windy, or what kind of day it was going to be. You just knew the sun will shine somewhere and when that went down the moon came up. But every day you stepped foot in Coach Hurley's gym, you had better be "*Chasing Perfect*."

2001-2002 Junior Varsity Team
Top: Carlos Colon, Atton Anderson, Otis Campbell, Christopher Frazier, Kristen Jacobs, Shelton Gibbs, Ahmad Mosby, Eduard Allen, Coach Carlos Cueto.
Bottom: Courtney Davis, Lamar Augustine, Thomas Hall, Justin Lewis, Todd Lawson, Rhodrick Allen.

Otis Campbell making a move to the basket.

2001-2002 Varsity Team
Top: Derrick Mercer, Reginald Smith, Lamar Alston, Obie Nwadike, Barney Anderson, Terrence Roberts, Patrick Reed, Wendell Bennett, Sean Bell, Sharif High, Isaiah George.

Bottom: Elijah Ingram, Shelton Gibbs, Marcus Williams, Quran Wimberly, Donald Copeland, Thomas Hall, Cheyenne Bostock, Dwayne Lee.

2001-2002 Center court celebration after winning the Tournament of Champions.

INTERVIEW V

Q: I felt like we all hit our breaking point at some time while playing for Coach Hurley. All maybe except Marcus. Would you guys say this is true?

Beanie: *That's a fact. Everybody hit a breaking point except Marcus. I don't know why Marcus didn't hit that breaking point. Maybe because he dealt with Coach Hurley prior to us, but when we had to deal with him! It was like.* **(Grabs his head with one hand)** *Good GOD!*

Marcus: *Nah, I never reached a breaking point with him. As far as him yelling at me, practice, or shit like that. I never reached that point. To me, I always took Coach Hurley as like a chess game. I always tried to stay one move ahead of him. That's how I took the whole game of basketball. To me it was like chess.* **(Laughing)** *Even though I never played chess.* **(Laughing)** *But I always heard you have to stay one step ahead of your opponent. Everything with him was like you have to know X, Y, and Z. That was the best thing for me to do. I knew every position and every play. He didn't have much of a reason to want to be upset with me. It was just like.* **(Paused)** *How do you stay off his bad side? I knew every position.*

Beanie. I remember you asking, how could you please someone that cannot be pleased, and you asked this question referring to Coach Hurley.

Q: What led you to this question?

Beanie: *Because it was like no matter what you did, somehow, someway, he found something wrong with it. So it's like in a game if we beating somebody by 30 points, he still found something wrong!* **(Imitating Coach Hurley's Voice) "You guys were soft today."** *It's like Coach, look at the score board. Isn't that the object of the game? To outscore your opponent!* **(Frowning face)** *It was just like there was always something wrong. You made a great play, but before that play, you on the court thinking like damn, if I fuck up it's going to be a sub. So you sitting there like,* *what can I do to make the perfect play? But the reality is, there is no perfect play with Coach Hurley. You still going to be wrong!* **(Laughing)**

Q: What was your most memorable kick out story?

Beanie: *When he kicked us all out because it was Valentine's Day.* **(Laughing)** *That was the worst of them all. He kicked one out and then he said you know what you leave too. The next thing you know, all of us was out of practice. It's like, what happened? Even though it was kind of like a relief, I'm not going to lie.* **(Laughing)** *We was like, yooo we get a break from practice! Still it was like damn Coach, what did you kick us out for?*

Otis: *I would have to say Valentine's Day. We walked in the gym Valentine's Day and he would have an attitude. We do one thing wrong.* **(Imitating Coach Hurley's Voice) "Up! You know what! All of you motherfuckers go with your girlfriends and go to the mall! Buy your girlfriends a card or something! Get the fuck out! It's Valentine's Day, you don't want to be here anyway! Get the fuck out!"** *Like that.* **(Laughing)** *There was this one time when we all were like, we not going to White Eagle today. Fuck that! It's nice outside, we ain't going! Even Marcus said it. We go to the gym the next day and Coach says,* **"Yeah, you guys decided not to come to White Eagle yesterday but your boy came!"** *Marcus's ass turned around, sneaky as hell, and goes to White Eagle without us. Coach says,* **"Yeah, he's the only smart one out of all you guys,"** *and kicks us out. Now we are looking at Marcus.* **(Paused)** *Like what the fuck! You just played us out. Snake the shit out of us.* **(Laughing)**

Marcus: *I never got kicked out of practice.*

Q: Marcus are you sure you never got kicked out of practice? I remember Coach kicking us out as a group?

Marcus: *I got kicked out because of y'all, because I was one of y'all. A lot of the shit I got in trouble for was because we all were together. No matter what, we all were together. Even if I didn't even do nothing. It was like, I'm a part of the crew.*

(Imitating Coach Hurley's Voice) "Marcus you get the fuck out with your crew!" *That's how it was. I only got kicked out because of y'all.*

Q: Is it safe to say that none of us really understood Coach Hurley's coaching methods? As far as his techniques he used as motivation, his criticism, and aggressiveness.

Beanie: *Nah, we didn't understand it because we were kids. We just liked playing. We were used to just playing, having fun, and we were winning. But when he was so demanding, it was just like we didn't understand it. Like Coach, we are going to win. We are going to be good enough. Why are you so demanding on us? But now that you look back on it, it was a reason behind it all.*

Marcus: *I could say I understood because I played for him two years before y'all did. Me as a freshman and sophomore, all the shit he was saying to the upperclassmen when I was younger, it was some of the same shit he was saying to us our junior and senior years. So I kind of knew where he was coming from with his motivation. Still, some of his methods didn't work with us as it would work with different type of kids maybe.*

Otis: *I didn't. I wasn't really trying to hear what he was saying. All I was thinking was that he didn't like me. Yelling at me all day. Fuck it, I quit. But they didn't let me quit. I brought my stuff to Sister Alan, she gave it back and said go to practice and deal with it. Once I got out of him yelling, and talking down, and trying to break me, I just focused on basketball. It made everything easier. Once I learned everything, the yelling stopped, the criticism stopped, everything stopped. It was just all about ball. I think that's what made me a better player for him because I was just focus on ball. I didn't worry about making a mistake and him yelling. He's going to yell anyway, but it wasn't bad at all my last year.*

Coach Hurley made me nervous at times. Nervous to mess up or to do certain things on the court.

Q: Did any of you feel that way?

Beanie: *Yes, because it seemed like he was never satisfied with anything you do. So in order for you to play, you had to play like you were perfect. In reality,* *basketball is a game of mistakes. If that was the case and the game was supposed to be perfect, there would never be an ending game. It would be a tie score every game. So it was kind of hard being out there because you want to do what you know you are capable of doing. Then again, you know if you try to do that and you mess up, you're coming out of the game. So you wanted to keep it as simple as possible.*

Marcus: *Hell Yeah! I was like that my first two years! After my first two years, I didn't give a shit. My freshman year was the worst. I still felt like I had a little cushion because I was only a freshman. When I got to junior and senior year, I felt like when I make a mistake, I make a mistake. After my first two years and now I'm a junior and senior, mistakes are going to happen. But my first two years I was scared to make every mistake possible. You make a mistake, you get out! That's it! You miss a fucking steal, you get out! Turnover, you get out!*

Otis: *Hell Yeah! Hell Yeah! Hell Yeah! I used to be scared to shoot. Scared to just be on the court, shit! You just have to go numb. You have to know that shit is going to happen. You are going to make mistakes. You're never going to have a perfect game and stuff is going to happen. Once I got rid of the nervousness, it was just like alright, I'm about to shoot from back here. You just got to play without that fear.*

Q: What's the difference between Coach Hurley and any other Coach you played for?

Beanie: *Freedom of playing. When you playing for Coach Hurley, you are in his system and in his element of play. When you play for any other coaches, they let you play within their element, but you also able to pretty much do some of the things that you know you can do. When you playing for Coach Hurley, those things are minimized. Such as certain moves, you know, certain things you would do. Certain passes. With Coach Hurley, no I'm not going to do that because if I do this and mess up, it might be bad for me. But when you played for the other coaches it was free will. If you did it and messed up they might have talked to you about it, but they would let you keep playing. They won't pull you out of the game, you won't be nervous, they'll let you redeem yourself pretty much. You make a bad play, they* *would let you make up for it by making a good play. Coach Hurley! You make a bad play, you coming out the game. It was a different comfort level.*

Marcus: *The discipline! The discipline and his methods. It was the best! Other coaches didn't have control over certain players. Coach Hurley had control over every player he had. Nobody tried to disrespect him! Nobody came at him sideways. Everybody paid attention and everybody listened and learned. You play with all these other coaches, you got coaches that don't know shit! I had a coach call me in the office and say,* **"What did y'all do at St. Anthony?"** *or,* **"What do you think we should do?"** *I'm like you're the coach! It was just that Coach Hurley, you know, he knew his shit. Everybody paid attention and everybody wanted to learn.*

Otis: *A lot of people can't play for Coach Hurley. What he says and feels is shown. You're not changing it at all. This coach might bend his rules a little. That coach might let you do everything it is that you want to do. But Coach Hurley! Nooo Buddy! It's his way and no other way. And his way is great. His way is the way that all the other coaches wanted.*

COACH HURLEY: THE DISCIPLINARY, THE PARENT, (THE GODFATHER)

Matthew Givens! There's a name you won't hear a lot when it comes to playing basketball at St. Anthony, but he was definitely in the mix. Matt played basketball with us going back to the early Boys & Girls Club days and even before then when we all as a group first really met, playing in CYO leagues against each other. Matt was my cousin and we grew up together. We always played ball for the same teams, but high school sophomore year is when he hung up his jersey as far as St. Anthony High School ball is concerned.

Matt, along with Beanie and I, dominated the St. Anthony freshmen team in 2000-2001, each scoring at least 20 points a game. I still tease them because I finished with MVP for the season. The streets had its way of getting around to you, and where you lived most certainly played a role on how fast you would be sucked in and fed to the wolves. Matt was a tremendous player and could have gone further but his attitude wouldn't let him get to the next level to play for Coach Hurley.

Coach Hurley was not your ordinary coach and there was no dictating your methods of basketball to him. Matt knew his attitude would not allow him to play for Coach Hurley and he knew that Coach Hurley would not tolerate any of the bullshit. He ended his basketball career with our 18-year-old AAU team and it was over from there. As we all went to college, Matt went to the "University of State Prison," along with Milly. Another player who started off at St. Anthony High School with our crew.

Milly was probably the best center in Jersey City around that time. If he could have kept his head on straight enough, Coach Hurley could have worked miracles with him and we all knew it. Not only did we know it, everyone in the city knew it. But if you read Coach Hurley's book, you would know that we were all stuck in our ways and some of us stuck in our ways a little too much. Coach Hurley had a few policies that every player had to follow in order to play for the St. Anthony's basketball team. You had to have a clean shaved face, clean haircut, and you were not allowed to get any tattoos while playing for the St. Anthony's program. Milly could not abide by the rules for some reason; he figured he was such a good player that Coach Hurley would bend the rules for him.

"Laughing my ass off," because little did he know, Coach Hurley didn't care if you were a better player than Michael Jordan himself, he was not bending his rules.

Now we all knew this before we decided to attend St. Anthony High. Milly, Matt, and I pushed it until the mere end to get haircuts. But for some reason Milly didn't want to cut his hair, and when he finally decided to cut it, he got caught bullying a kid for his radio. The kid ended up telling on him the next day in school and Milly was kicked out. Funny, I think that kid ended up transferring out of the school because we kind of put pressure on him for being a snitch. He knew that was against the rules. After all, "Snitches Get Stitches." Just like Coach Hurley, we weren't going to bend our rules either, at least with any of our peers.

Before Milly could even put on a St. Anthony's practice uniform, he was already shipped out of the school like a package that had been delivered to the wrong place. Milly had a good three and a half years at Snyder High School and suddenly he quit his senior year. Not too long afterwards he ended up getting arrested for armed robbery. He was one of our brothers and it hit us all hard because we had the power to persuade him to do the right things. If he had just stayed at St. Anthony with us, it would have been easier for us to reach out to him. He got close to a 20-year sentence and is still serving his time now.

If you have heard anything about Coach Hurley, you know that he is not just a basketball coach. He is a life coach, teacher, mentor, role model, father figure, and so on. With all that being said, being a good father figure means he took on the role of molding you into a young man that has respect for yourself and others. A man that takes pride in what you do and holds his head high. So the rough edges had to be straightened out, and he would straighten them out the best he could. However, it didn't only fall on him; you had to be able to receive his disciplinary tactics the proper way. That was the hard part. That was the part Matt and Milly wasn't able to endure.

Coach Hurley's disciplinary tactics could very well be taken the wrong way. Things that he did or said would really make you wonder if he had your best interest at heart or not. One with a weak mind would be broken. As teenagers, we didn't understand these methods because all we wanted to do is play basketball. That's all we ever wanted to do. So when Coach Hurley tells you that you'll never be as good as the players who previously left the school, you either take it for the good or for the bad. You sit, think, and say damn he doesn't think I'm a good player. Or, you say man fuck that, I'm going to prove him wrong. Now you have your motivation.

The very first part of falling in line and being disciplined didn't even start while we were students at St. Anthony High School. This started in elementary school. Coach Hurley had influence on your life in elementary school. The teachers knew who was going to St. Anthony High School and they knew who played sports. Otis and I were constantly told by our eighth-grade math teacher that we had better straighten up if we were going to St. Anthony and planned on playing basketball. Mr. Broncado was his name and I'm not sure if the spelling is right, but I remember him clearly telling us that.

"Otis, you think you're going to attend St. Anthony High School with an attitude like that and play for Coach Bob Hurley? Oh noooooo buddy, That's Bologna!" (As he waved his hands at Otis) "You're going to go there and be jumping off the walls, and you know what Coach Hurley is going to say! Get out of my gym, Go home!" He then looked at me and said, "Shelton, you should be fine if you don't let yourself get distracted, but you guys have a rude awakening coming your way if you think you're going to St. Anthony and running things."

This was in eighth-grade as Otis was acting out in class and I began to laugh. In the middle of class our math teacher brought up basketball and Coach Hurley's program at St. Anthony High School. At the time, I was like wow, how does he know about Coach Hurley and the basketball program? Yet, now I realize how much this amazing coach had already built a successful basketball power house.

Gary Greenberg, who played a major role in all of our decisions on going to St. Anthony High School, told us that we would have to cut our hair, have clean faces, no tattoos, and no piercings. We asked why and we originally thought it was because we were going to a Catholic high school, but Milly and I found out why that summer before high school when we were at Coach Hurley's Pocono Basketball Camp.

Coach Hurley's basketball camps were great, we had so much fun going there as kids. You got to stay in a cabin full of your friends, learn, and compete with players from everywhere. For the average kid out of Jersey City, that was the ultimate summer vacation. Playing basketball, hanging out with your homeboys, and learning from Coach Bob Hurley along with his basketball team. We had been going to Coach's camp for several years, but it wasn't until eighth-grade summer when we had our very first disciplinary session from Coach Hurley himself.

It was the last day of camp and we were running around the camp going wild having a blast. It was time for everyone to go home and our rides hadn't arrived yet, so we wandered off and began to goof around.

Milly and I saw one of the golf carts in the cut and most of the camp staff were gone. We got a screwdriver, put it in the ignition, and started it up. We started driving around the camp having a blast in the golf cart, and I ended up getting stuck in a pile of mud.

I yelled, "Oh shit Milly, we stuck bro!"

Milly responded, "Fuck that man we out, let's go!"

I said, "Nah, just get in the driver's seat and keep hitting the gas. I'm going to jump in the mud and push. Fuck that, I'm not trying to get in trouble!"

Milly hops in the driver's seat and began to hit the gas as I just kept pushing and pushing until finally the golf cart frees up. I quickly told Milly we needed to put the golf cart back and go get lost. Now as we were putting it back we noticed a few of our Boys & Girls Club teammates at the snack shack just having a free for all. So what do we do? Yup, we join the party and get our free snacks. Not even realizing that they got the free snacks because they vandalized the damn snack shack area. Now we crashed the damn golf cart, became accessories to vandalizing the snack shack and taking snacks, yet still managed not to get caught.

Okay, now we have our free snacks, put the golf cart back, and headed to the playing area where a few staff members are still left playing pool. We joined the pool game and one of our teammates was playing around with one of the staff members. One thing leads to another and the staff takes a pool stick and shoves it in the kid's ass. Now if he didn't know any better, he was about to find out why you don't do shit like that to any kid from the hood of Jersey City. Whether he was playing or not, that was a violation in our book.

Keep in mind that we lived by the no snitching rule. We weren't about to run and tell that this young adult is sticking a pool stick up an eighth-grader's ass. So, Milly and I grabbed the guy off of our teammate and threw him on the floor. As we got him on the floor, we began kicking and punching him. At this point all the fun and games were over.

Our other teammates jumped in and began beating him up too. The staff ended up running off. A bunch of 12 and 13-year-old's beating up an adult as if he wasn't one of our elders. Well, respect your elders went right out the window on this one.

Shortly after Coach Hurley approaches us and he's not approaching with a pleasant look on his face. Because of my dad, I have had several conversations with Coach as an even younger kid which I was 12 years old at the time, and he was always welcoming. This moment I got to see the disciplinary part of Coach Hurley for the very first time.

"All of you come over here and sit on this bench. NOW! What the fuck is wrong with you guys! You have the nerve to beat up one of my staff, are you shitting me!"

I attempted to say something and all I could get to was, "but Coa..." and I was cut off immediately.

"SHUT UP WHILE I AM TALKING! You guys had better get your acts together if you plan on coming to St. Anthony! That behavior is unacceptable! What would even make you think to harm one of my staff? MY STAFF! And guess what, the braids on your heads, cut them off come school time! You guys are going to have clean low-cut haircuts, shaved faces, and clear arms! If you have a problem with it, you can pick another school! The shit you guys pulled just now will not happen. My staff runs to me, telling me that you guys jumped on him! Are you fucking kidding me! You will be clean cut newly groomed young men! Everyone get your shit and go to the front to wait for your rides! HURRY UP!"

We all quickly got up and rushed to the path that the cars came to and waited for our ride. That fucking snake of a staff ran and told on us, but kept vital information out. As we sat in the road we discussed our options. We can kick his ass again for doing what he just did and fuck going to St. Anthony, we can go to Marist High School. Or, we can just be glad that we didn't get yelled at for that golf cart and that damn snack shack.

Angrily, we went with option two because LORD knows we wanted to kick his ass again.

This was the beginning of four more years of dealing with this method of discipline. I mean you could at least give an explanation as to what happened to your parents, even to any other coaches we played for, but not Coach Hurley. Oh no, there was no explanation for anything. Even if he asked you for one, there was still no explanation to give. His explanation was the only explanation that was acceptable.

In high school or in any school you know exactly what you need to do when you are there. Go to school, pay attention in class, learn, become educated, and so on. In elementary school, it was just that and if you acted out your parent or parents were called in. In St. Anthony same thing, but on top of that, Coach Hurley was informed as well. We gained two additional parents at St. Anthony. Not only did we have to deal with our parents, we had to deal with our second parent Coach Hurley, and then our third parent who was the wonderful Sister Alan.

If you got in any trouble in school, getting put on punishment from your parents at home wasn't enough. You got disciplined by Coach Hurley the parent next. At that point, you never really wanted to get into anything at all in school, but for us that was extremely impossible. Just think of trouble as candy, and our crew Matt, Beanie, Otis, Marcus, Milly, Lamar, and me are the kids that loved candy. Well anything you do with a kid that loves candy won't steer him away from it, especially when you have your back turned.

St. Anthony was our candy store and the only parent that you didn't worry about was Sister Alan. She was the buffer. After you got it from the first two sets of parents, Sister Alan came to you kindly and warm-heartedly. She let you hear it, but the way she did it was so calm and welcoming that it didn't feel like you were in trouble. At the end, you got a gentle rub on the top of your back and were told to do better.

Yet, that gentle rub from Sister Alan could only go so far because it never seemed like we could stay away from trouble. We were all just a bunch of knuckleheaded daredevils. Beanie could never get away from the do-rag trouble, that was a given. We all wore do-rags at the time, it was the thing. You brush your hair, put some wave grease in your head, and try to get what we called 360 waves. You needed waves all around your head because the girls liked that. The girls liked the waves so much they would just rub on your head all day and say, "Ewww look at them waves," and Beanie had the waves.

Thing is, some of the teachers and counselors wouldn't even give you a chance to take the damn do-rag off before they jumped down your back. Some days they would be standing at the door when you were coming into school just waiting for someone to walk in with a do-rag on. The second you stepped in the door, it was take off that do-rag now. Next came the threats to tell Coach Hurley. They used that to control us and it was annoying. So annoying that one-day Beanie snapped.

Mr. Ed Szalkiewicz saw Beanie with his do-rag on and just like everyone would do, he asked Beanie to take it off. Beanie would have easily taken the do-rag off with no problem. Yet, instead of just a simple take it off, what does Mr. Szalkiewicz say, "I'm going to call Coach Hurley." The school staff didn't seem to have their own back bone and they always used Coach Hurley to control his players. The smallest thing would lead to the teacher saying they would call Coach Hurley. Oh, you yawned and didn't say excuse me, "I'm going to call Coach Hurley." Hey, your sneakers aren't tied, "I'm going to call Coach Hurley." You, you missed the garbage can and threw garbage on the floor, "I'm going to call Coach Hurley."

This got frustrating with all of us, but this day Beanie must have been having a hard day. Maybe with his girlfriend or at home. So instead of him just taking the do-rag off, he snapped.

"Go ahead, I don't care."

As he kept walking away from Mr. Szalkiewicz, Coach Darren Erman, who is now an Assistant Coach in the NBA, overheard and approached the situation to calm Beanie down. Coach Erman could get this done with no problem. He was one of the good guys. As a team we had the utmost respect for Coach Erman because of his background and how he carried himself. Coach Erman worked at a law firm prior to coming to St. Anthony, probably making over 100,000 dollars a year. He left that to come to St. Anthony High School and help coach a group of knuckle-headed kids like us. We all knew that he definitely took a huge pay cut because as we learn from the gangsters in our city and teachers in school, lawyers get paid the big bucks.

Coach Erman wasn't like the other coaches. He was very easily approachable, he was just so damn happy to be around Coach Hurley and this program and it showed. Instead of us seeing him as a coach, we saw him as a big brother because he didn't look that old and he would talk to us in a way that no other coach would. It wouldn't get back to Coach Hurley and he wouldn't threaten us with, "I'm going to call Coach Hurley." When he approached Beanie, it wasn't the same as Mr. Szalkiewicz approaching him. Still, this led Beanie to being suspended from the team.

Now to the school staff and coaches this might have seemed to be another Beanie acting out moment. Yet, the truth to the entire matter was that Mr. Szalkiewicz just had to say, "I'm going to call Coach Hurley." This outburst could have come from any of us at any given moment and with each of us it would have been a different reaction. We knew why Beanie disregarded the request to take his do-rag off, and it wasn't for any other reason but the fact he was just tired of the "I'm going to call Coach Hurley" threats. We all were.

This reminded me of a similar incident that happened with me when we were playing freshman basketball for Coach Tony DiGiovanni. However, he didn't threaten to call Coach Hurley, he kind of mimicked Coach Hurley's techniques. Right before practice Matt, Beanie, and I walked into the gym and it was cold outside. I always liked wearing chains, it was my thing. I had my skull cap on my head with a do-rag underneath it. As we all walked into the gym I zipped my coat down, still shaking and blowing into my hands to try to warm up. Now my long chain is showing, I have on a skull cap, and a do-rag.

Coach DiGiovanni begins to go off.

"Oh, what do you think you are some kind of rapper or something, take that fucking skull cap and do-rag off in the gym."

Now as he is saying this I heard exactly what he was saying and remind you this was just our freshman year. Already we found out that Coach Hurley was "The Godfather" because everyone either tried to mimic him or threatened to call him. Yet, Coach DiGiovanni managed to quickly turn my good mood into frustration and anger.

I shouted back in anger.

"What! What you say? I think I'm a rapper! What kind of racist shit is that to say you racist motherfucker! It's cold as hell outside and yeah, I still have my fucking hat on! Not because I'm trying to disrespect the rules, but I'm trying to keep warm. You are talking this racist bullshit! Fuck You!"

Now I didn't think Coach DiGiovanni was racist at all. It was the way he made the statement that made me feel like he was judging me. I felt like he was trying to mimic Coach Hurley and it came out the wrong way. I was sure I would hear it the next day and be suspended. Somehow, the next day when I came to practice things had started and ended normal. No interaction with Coach Hurley, no revisit of the day before, and no suspension. I had a new-found respect for Coach DiGiovanni. He didn't tell Hurley on me, nor did my parents find out. At least I don't think none of that happened, but I apologized and told him I didn't at all think he was racist. I told him about how I felt everyone acted like Coach Hurley, and he talked back to me like a mentor.

Coach Hurley was "The Godfather" and I called him that because he called all the shots. He called the shots on the court, off the court, and everywhere else for that matter. Wherever you went, someone knew Coach Hurley and things had the possibility of getting back to him. So we had to be sneakier than usual if we did anything we weren't supposed to be doing.

It's funny because I remember Coach Hurley enforcing curfew on us. His curfew was earlier than some of the curfews our parents gave us. Our home parents because remember Coach Hurley was our parent as well. He made it very clear as we entered the school freshman year that he was our mothers and our fathers for the next four years. I think his curfew was 9 o'clock and some of us had 10 o'clock curfews on certain days. Shit, I don't think Marcus had a curfew because this guy was out all night.

I can recall one-night Marcus and I were out past curfew on Ocean Avenue. I think Coach had a white Toyota at the time and all we saw was a white Toyota driving on Ocean Avenue. We quickly ran and began to hide. As the Toyota drove past, it sure as hell was Coach Hurley. Marcus and I looked at each other and started shaking our heads. Marcus then said, "Yo, this motherfucker ain't playing," and I responded, "No he's not." Coach Hurley lived all the way on the other side of town, so in our minds he had to be driving around making sure we weren't out on the streets. Occasionally, we would see Coach Gamble's jeep come riding around and we would expect that because he lived in the area. For Coach Hurley to come riding around, it really showed his dedication.

It seemed like Coach Hurley would always be on our backs and at times we became down. Like I said, he was more than just a coach, therefore it was way more to things than just basketball. School was important. Coach would reiterate this to us all the time. "You guys are student athletes," he would say. Getting into trouble in school or outside school was frowned upon.

In Ms. Patel's Science class, we had some pretty strong science equipment that was not meant to be played with unless the teachers told us to. Of course, when the teacher explained the strength of some of these objects and told us not to play with them, it made us even more curious. Now what does Otis decide to do. He takes this glue that supposedly was very strong and anything that it touched would stick to it.

Otis puts the glue on the teacher's chair, on her pet rock, and on the door knob to leave the classroom. Ms. Patel had a routine every morning. She would come in the class, sit in her chair, and kiss her pet rock. The class just so happened to be right next door to my class and I knew what Otis was planning to do. I asked for a pass to the bathroom and went next door to sit in on the action.

Ms. Patel walked into the class and said good morning. Just as she did every morning, she followed her routine. I catch myself speaking aloud saying no way in hell is this glue that strong. Ms. Patel sat down and grabbed her pet rock lifting it to her lips to kiss it. As she proceeded to put the rock down and lift her hand up, the rock was still stuck to parts of her hand.

She yelled out, "WHATS THIS? WHATS GOING ON?" She then proceeded to stand and her clothing was stuck to the chair. "YOU GUYS WERE PLAYING WITH THAT GLUE! OH MY GOSH I CAN'T BELIEVE THIS! WHO WOULD DO THIS?" She wobbled to the door to exit the classroom grabbing the door knob. This couldn't get any better. As she grabbed the door with the rock stuck to her hand and the chair to her back, she quickly realized that she had just grabbed onto more glue with her other hand.

"ARE YOU FREAKING KIDDING ME!"

The entire classroom laughed so hard but in the next few minutes' things weren't going to be so funny. I knew this so I went right back next door to my original classroom. I heard a teacher yelling and all I could do was laugh. Otis played the biggest prank ever, but he made the mistake of doing this while too many eyes were around. Later on in practice, Coach Hurley called us to the center of the court.

"So today in school, OTIS FUCKING CAMPBELL decides to glue the teachers hand to her pet rock! Instead of going to school, getting an education, and doing what he is supposed to do, Otis is in class goofing around. Now who does this hurt? You guys because he's suspended!"

I was just waiting on him to kick me out because someone told him I was in the classroom. When he finished talking and didn't call my name I knew I was cleared. Yet again, Coach had to discipline us and by our senior year I think he pretty much had enough. We would constantly be caught in bullshit and maybe it was because Coach Hurley was so demanding of us.

We had to dress differently, act differently, and do everything differently than our peers who weren't playing basketball. When the school day was over we had to go to study hall while our friends that didn't play basketball got to hang in the mall. If we were late or skipped, we got punished. We had to go to SAT prep classes when we weren't in study hall. All the other students got to go home to chill, but we had to be in class and behave even after school was over.

Pre-Season in SAT classes we were goofing around and of course the teacher informed Coach Hurley of our actions. When Coach got to us, he again let us have it. He let us know that we weren't the senior class that he wanted the underclassmen to look up to. We weren't the students that we were supposed to be. He also let us know, that as much as we wanted to get away from him, he and the coaching staff had that same feeling towards us.

Coach Hurley was right, he was 100% right. We were definitely bad influences on the underclassmen. We also had no intentions on leading them or being role models to them. We had other things we were interested in. In all of our minds we just wanted to get through each day the fastest, slickest, and easiest way we could. Go to school, go to practice, then try to get home safely without getting into any shit in the streets. To hell with anything else. Still after it all, we wanted to do what we wanted to do.

At this point we were still getting into all the bullshit in the streets. Coach Hurley could try all he wanted, but he didn't have to go home with us. I honestly think that if we didn't have so much shit going on that we could have pulled together and been the crew everyone wanted us to be. Yet, things were getting heated in the streets.

Several students from our school were granted the opportunity to go to a golf outing where we sold raffle tickets to raise money for school. Before we even got to the outing we were planning on how we would swindle extra tickets for ourselves and keep money. Let's take some of the other kid's tickets we thought. Better yet, let's act like we are comparing tickets sold and sneak twenty here, forty there. Marcus wanted to provide for his son, Otis wanted clothes, and I wanted the gun that I referred to in the earlier chapters.

Seven of us from the team got the chance to go. Sean, Qaysir, Derrick, Barney, Otis, Marcus, and me. Now here is how that bad influence on the underclassman came to be a part of all this. Barney and Derrick had no idea we planned this, but they caught on. I proceeded to do what I thought was a good idea. One ticket was twenty dollars, and a stack of seven would allow you to get two tickets free priced at 100 dollars. Instead of me telling the buyers that information, I told them one for twenty and once I got 100 dollars I would keep the extra two tickets as if I sold a stack of seven. This would give me forty dollars for every two tickets I would keep.

I did that until I got the amount of money I needed for the gun. Marcus and Otis were doing what they were doing. They didn't have a method; they were just taking money. The next thing you know Derrick and Barney were taking money. Which then led to every kid that went to the damn event to take at least twenty dollars. Every kid except for one girl. All I could think was, what the fuck did we start? This wasn't the right thing to do at all and I knew it. Yet, my fear of something happening to me in the streets overwhelmed me and I kept the money.

We got on the bus after a busy day and I was scared because this thing had gotten out of control. Those guys didn't think like I thought, I thought about the consequences we would face, shit I would face. My parents were strict; my dad was going to kill me if he knew I was involved. Coach Hurley would kick us off the fucking team. I never wanted to return money so damn fast.

On the bus ride home, Marcus is now flashing money.

"I got like 500 dollars yo, my son going to be good."

Otis would laugh and respond, "I got like 400 son. I'm going to the mall tomorrow."

Of course, I was sitting next to the girl that had nothing and I was already scared so I pretended I didn't know anything about what was going on. I looked at her and said, "Man, they wilding out." After they started to show off their money, the next thing you know everyone else started too. It was a shit show from there. I knew this would get back to Coach Hurley one way or another and now I was thinking about how the hell I was going to get out of this situation.

The girl next to me looked so disgusted and I felt the way that she looked. I wasn't happy with myself at all, I shouldn't have done this. I told everyone to shut up before the bus driver told on them, as I still acted as if I didn't take anything myself. I just knew this girl next to me was definitely going to tell. We just did a terrible thing.

The same night I took the money straight to the guy that was selling the gun; I told him I would have the money by the end of the night. I didn't want to keep him waiting because I was nervous he might do something. I told him I was coming with some guys and they would be waiting for me so he didn't know I was alone. He gave me the gun and I went home to hide the gun in the ceiling.

In school the next day I was on edge. I just knew Coach Hurley would be at the school. I was so nervous and sure enough the intercom sounded.

"Will Otis Campbell, Shelton Gibbs, Marcus Williams, Derrick Mercer, and Barney Anderson report to the office immediately?"

I just knew we were all in deep shit. We got to the office where Sister Alan was waiting and she was so pissed. I had never seen Sister Alan so pissed in all my time at St. Anthony.

"All of you are to call your parents and have them come to the school tonight. We have a meeting with Coach Hurley. You all decided to steal money from the golf outing, you should be ashamed of yourselves, all of you!"

I knew I was in deep shit and at this point I knew damn well I couldn't tell my father I was involved in this. He was going to kill me. My father always told me I didn't need to steal anything. He also told me that if I wanted something, I should work for it or ask him. What I wanted I couldn't ask for and I had never asked for that amount of money before, otherwise I would have asked and lied about what it was for.

We got together and the initial game plan was to deny, deny, deny everything. We didn't take anything. There was no way that they could know exactly how much we took, so we planned on seeing if they said numbers and go from there. Coach Hurley was standing in the middle of the classroom and all of our parents were there. Oh man was I so nervous, this was a nightmare and I didn't want to be kicked out or in trouble.

"The reason we are here is because we had a golf outing and your kids stole money!"

Our parents quickly got offended and began to blurt things back.

"My son didn't steal anything, I asked him and he told me he didn't take nothing!"

"Well how much money did they supposedly take?"

The questions and comments kept going. Coach Hurley responded.

"Listen, I know it may be hard to believe. But the fact of the matter is some of the kids in here already stood up and confessed. They told us everything already. At this point you guys need to come forward and be honest. There is nothing that upsets me more than not being able to stand up and take responsibility for your actions. It's pathetic!"

Coach Hurley was disgusted, and I don't know how the other guys felt but I felt like shit. If I wasn't afraid my father was going to kill me, I would have come forward and confessed myself. Coach Hurley left, Sister Alan went over the dollar amounts, and all of the dollar amounts were off. They didn't know how much we took and if nobody would have said anything they probably wouldn't have even known.

Of course the girl I was sitting next to initially told on us, and when Derrick and Barney were confronted they confessed. They even asked the bus driver and she said she didn't know what was going on, even though I knew she knew. I saw her looking in her mirror shaking her head as she drove, but even she didn't tell.

Here we were again in some shit we had no business being into. We were knuckleheads, we were bad influences, we were definitely the worst group of kids that Coach Hurley ever had to coach. I felt like shit, our parents had to pay back the amounts of money they said we stole. Coach Hurley suspended us from the team and made us do 100 hours of community service before we were allowed back.

My parents tried to get me to confess because part of them believed I didn't take anything. Whether I took money or not, my father knew for sure that even if I didn't take money, I knew who did and I wasn't going to tell. He knew how tight our friendship was and telling on each other was not something we were going to do.

This ended up being covered up with saying we were starting trouble on the bus. We were assholes, we were everything that Coach Hurley called us. We tried to stray away from everything we were around, but we became exactly what we were trying not to become. Products of our environments.

I was sure Coach Hurley would give up on us at this point, but he gave us another chance. There was something that he saw, maybe he knew that if he completely gave up on us we would be lost to the streets. Instead of allowing us to self-destruct, he continued to stay on us. He continued to mold us into the young men he felt we could be. If our parents didn't hold us to a certain standard, he didn't care. We had better perform to Coach Hurley's standards.

Coach Hurley was not only there for us as a second parent or just a disciplinary figure, he protected us as well. There were several times the Jersey City roughness was almost driven out of him. You could tell this man was no push over and he didn't take shit from anyone. If anyone got out of line and did anything disrespectful towards us, he stepped in and said something. He didn't turn a blind eye or back down, it wasn't in him. He himself knew what it was like growing up in Jersey City.

There were several games when Coach Hurley had to step in and calm the games down. He didn't allow us to retaliate if a player got too rough with us. If we did, he took us out of the game right away. He expected us to play with class and with honor. Yet, every so often he had to say something to the refs. Both of his hands would go up into the air and he would place them on his head as he walked onto the court.

"LISTEN GUYS, YOU HAVE TO DO A BETTER JOB CONTROLLING THE GAME! I DON'T KNOW HOW LONG I CAN CONTROL THESE GUYS FROM RETALIATING TO THE SHIT SHOW YOU'RE ALLOWING OUT HERE. THEY ARE KILLING MY GUYS! GET CONTROL OF THE GAME!!!"

His voice was always so stern and traveled through the entire gym. It seemed as if everyone got his drift and it was just so amazing to me that this man would literally just walk all the way on the court as if a game wasn't going on at all. Yet, he was understood loud and clear.

From the outside looking in, people thought Coach Hurley was too harsh on us and they always had an opinion.

"Oh, he needs to calm down."

"Those boys are in boot camp with that Coach."

"He's yelling at them and they are up by 30."

"He's worse than Coach Bob Knight."

A whole bunch of talk but no one understood. He had to be tough on us. It was the only way possible that we would get anything accomplished. If he wasn't on us the way he was, we would get too relaxed and wouldn't have worked as hard as we did. Still, there was something about that Bob Knight comment that he didn't like and in the middle of a game one of the opponent's parents were yelling out to him. Taunting him the entire game.

"Bobby Knight! Why don't you leave the kids alone!"

"Hey Bobby Knight, you're winning why don't you take it easy on them!"

"Bobby Knight, you want to hit one of the kids don't you!"

"Bobby Knight, Bobby Knight, Bobby Knight!"

Well I guess enough was enough and Coach Hurley almost lost it. He turned into the crowd and walked up to the bleachers. As he stared in the crowd and rolled up his sleeves his voice travelled, "YOU WANT A PIECE OF ME? DO YOU WANT A PIECE OF ME?" We all looked and was surprised. I remember thinking to myself, wow the Jersey City is coming out of Coach. The other coaches grabbed Coach Hurley and talked him down. Coach Hurley was just like us. One thing about growing up in the hood of Jersey City, "The apple doesn't fall far from the tree."

INTERVIEW VI

Q: How did you feel about someone always using the, "I'm going to tell Coach Hurley" line?

Beanie: *I hated it. I hated it with a passion! It was like this, Hurley is Hurley and you are you. Two different people. Why are you even trying to be like him and then you use the comment, "Oh, I'm going to tell Bob?" It's just even more frustrating. You're going to tell Coach Hurley, he's going to yell at me, but in reality, what are you getting out of it? You're still not going to have the control. He is going to have the control because I want to play basketball and he is my coach. So now, you are telling me you are going to tell Bob, I'm looking at you like well who are you as the adult here? You have to tell another adult? Then you must have not established respect for yourself. Coach Hurley is the person I respect because he broke that barrier down, like you are going to respect me!*

Marcus: *That shit went in one ear and out the other. It didn't really mean nothing to me. The teachers in school used it as a scare tactic. That shit ain't scare me. You are saying it because you think it's going to scare me into doing what you want, but it didn't matter.*

Otis: *I wasn't worried about that. What were they going to tell Hurley that my chair was stationed in the hallway during my Spanish class? He knew that! I knew that! I was never really worried about it but just hearing it all the time was the frustrating part.*

Q: When Milly was kicked out of St. Anthony, what were your thoughts on that?

Beanie: *I was messed up by it because he was a part of the circle. He was a part of the crew. And like I said, we all played together, we stuck together. Whatever happened outside of school, we stuck together and it was like not for nothing, sometimes we kept each other out of certain situations. So when he got kicked out of St. Anthony, we couldn't really keep up with him like we used to. We tried to hang with* *him, but we couldn't. That's when he started to fall from the path and take his own route. It bothered me a lot because we lost one of our brothers.*

Marcus: *When he got kicked out it hurt me because we were from the same place. We both grew up in the projects, we did everything together me and him. It hurt me. I was trying to talk to him to stay in the right direction, but he didn't want to do that. He didn't want to cut his braids. I don't think St. Anthony was for Milly. Milly had the Curries Woods, Snyder mentality in him from the jump. Everybody played for the Boys Club so we all felt like St. Anthony was the place to go. Milly figured if everybody is going, I'm going. We are all going to stick together, so I think that's what made his decision for him. But I don't think that's where he really wanted to be at. It hurt me that he wasn't with us.*

Otis: *It was a hurtful feeling to see one of my brothers off the team and I couldn't play with him. St. Anthony is not for everybody. I feel like you have to be an elite, strong individual to play or be there because you're going to go through a lot. Shit if you going to break easily, that ain't the spot for you. If your mentality is not good or you are easy to be broken, don't go there.*

Q: How did you feel when Milly quit the Snyder High School Team?

Beanie: *I think they beat Bloomfield Tech that year! I was just like Whoooaaa! What is he doing? You left here and then you went somewhere that you felt you were in your comfort zone. Somewhere that you were around a lot more people that you grew up with from where you lived at. You were doing your thing. Great! Why not stick to it? For you to quit the team, it was just like.* **(Paused)** *LORD knows. What is he going to do now? But I feel like if we all were still together, I don't think that would have happened.*

Otis: *He had to go to night school because he was short on credits to graduate on time. He wanted to graduate on time, so he went to night school and that was his decision he had to make. He didn't want to do another year in high school so he had to quit. I think that's what influenced a lot of his decisions after that because he didn't have ball no more.*

Marcus: *I was upset! He never told me a reason. What Otis said was my first time hearing any reason. I thought he just led to the streets and got sucked in. I never heard a story from him or anybody else as to why he quit, why he stopped playing. I never knew. Maybe he lost love for the game, but I don't know the reason he stopped playing.*

Q: How did you feel when Milly was arrested and sentenced to so many years in prison?
Beanie: *I felt like he got introduced to another route and got sucked right in. He couldn't see the way out of that life. It was over from there.* ***(Shaking Head)***
Marcus: *At the end of the day. Every decision a person makes is their own decision. That's something he had to live with. I lived with it too, not seeing my friend anymore. Hopefully when he comes back he can make the best out of being away from his friends, family, his daughter. Do things the right way. I think he was sentenced to 15 years or more. A long time. A very long time.*
Otis: *I was like what the hell did he do! I was in school at the time in Kansas. When I got the news, there was nothing I can do. I still talked to Milly. We wrote letters, he sent me a couple of pictures and let me know that he was good. I didn't know what else to do.*

Beanie. You were the Do-Rag King. I remember Mr. Szalkiewiez yelling at you about your do-rag.
Q: Was there anything besides the do-rag that was bothering you that day when you exploded on him?
Beanie: *First of all, I almost got stuck in the house with my nephew again because of my sister. Then on top of that, I didn't even have no lunch money! I was hungry! And then I had to walk to school on top of that. I was rushing to get to school on time. I got to school! On time! As I'm running to my class you hear somebody, "TAKE YOUR DO-RAG OFF!" I kept going. I, I kept going. I made it to class. As soon as I sit down, I made it to class and I decided I'm taking my do-rag off.* ***"I'm telling Coach Hurley."*** *What? Back to the beginning, that's the trigger again. You're not Bob Hurley and at that, I still took my do-rag off. So I didn't understand*

what I did wrong. I was rushing to make it on time and I still made it on time. I don't know if you were having a bad morning or you just decided, I'm going to pick at Beanie today because he is running through the hallway with his do-rag. Trying to make it to class on time.

Q: I felt like we all had respect for Coach Darren Erman, would you guys agree?

Beanie: *Yeah, 100%. He was young and he understood. We could go and talk to Darren and we didn't have to worry about it getting nowhere. Didn't get back to Coach Hurley, Coach Gamble, it wouldn't got to nobody. It would be between you and him and he would talk to you about it. Then he would check up with you the next day to see what's going on with you still. He was different. He was a good dude.*

Marcus: *I had respect for Coach Erman. He wanted to follow a dream and he gave up his life, his career, to come to St. Anthony basically for nothing. I think he was living in White Eagle Hall or whatever. He was willing to learn and he was there for us. He was a cool guy.*

Otis: *Errrrrrmmm! Yeah, I had respect for him. He was young, he didn't care if he slept in his car. All he wanted to do was learn the game. That's why he is successful now, because he put that time and effort in. He took a loss early to make up for it in the end. I have nothing but love for Erman. He used to say,* **"I'm in the same boat as you guys." (Laughing)**

Q: Coach Hurley was a very stern Coach. Do you think you could talk back to Coach Hurley, or give him an explanation to anything?

Beanie: *Nah! Emm Emm. It was what he says goes! That's it. Nothing else behind it. You can't even say, Coach but I thought this. NO! NO! You're wrong.*

Marcus: *Nah, it was his way or the highway. Whether you felt as though you were right, it was whatever he says is going to go. In your heart and mind, you got to know you made your best decision for yourself. There were no answers to give him, you just go to the next play.*

Otis: *Hell no! It's like talking back to your moms! You're never going to be right in that situation. He had a way of making you feel like, why the fuck you even say anything back to him. Now you're being disrespectful. Now you think you smarter than me. You know more than me.*

This is a very sensitive subject for me and I don't know how you guys feel about it. If there was ever anything that I regretted doing during our time at St. Anthony, that was taking that money from the golf tournament.

Q: I ask honestly, how did you guys feel at the time we were doing that? How do you feel now?

Marcus: *Back then, it was an entirely different situation back then. Times were rough for certain people. When we did that I regretted it right away because it took a toll on the team. On us as individuals. On our parents. If I could go back I would change and do things the right way.*

Otis: *At the time, I was thinking about what type of sneakers I was going to get. I lied in my mother's face and I lied in Coach Hurley's face. Today I feel like we definitely shouldn't have did it. I wouldn't do anything like that now. At all! At that point in time everybody had separate problems. It was wrong, we shouldn't have done that.*

THE UPPERCLASSMEN

THERE ARE TIMES when you enter a new school and you hear previous stories about the upperclassmen with their hazing tactics. They make the new players shave their heads or dye their hair. Make them do something stupid that will land them in the principal's office or in detention. Coming into St. Anthony High School as freshmen, we didn't know what to expect. All we knew was that we weren't going to be hazed or bullied around by anyone.

We quickly learned about "Tag Day" in St. Anthony our freshmen year. Tag Day was a day you got to come to school and wear anything you wanted to wear. This was a day you could wear hats in school and dress in street clothes, since normally we wore uniforms to school. Everyone would wear their best outfit they had in their closet at home. Tag Day was like Easter Sunday for us because usually on Easter your parents would buy you a brand-new Easter outfit to look nice. Well on Tag Day you would come in wearing your very best.

At the time, Coogi sweaters were very popular and all the kids had to have them just to show off. If you didn't come to school in a Coogi you were considered a nobody. It was like a fashion show in school, everybody walking around showing off their clothing like they were ripping the runway. Basketball season hadn't even started when we had our first Tag Day. A senior came up to me and whispered a little something in my ear, "Yo, I like your Coogi. I'm going to take it from you by the end of the day, you watch." He said this to me as he tugged on my sweater.

Now I didn't know if he was joking or not, but I didn't take it as a joke. I came from a rough neighborhood and if someone in my area told me something like that, it wasn't interpreted as a joke. I told Milly, Matt, Otis, and the rest of the crew about what happened. When I told them, I wasn't intending for it to turn into a big thing, but by after school it was. As the last period bell rang they were outside already waiting for the kid to come out. "Which one of them said they were going to take your Coogi?" Milly asked. As the kid came outside I pointed him out.

We were freshman at the time and there was no way we would stand the taunting or anything else from the upperclassman. We weren't going to deal with bullshit in school then go home and deal with bullshit in the streets. As I pointed the kid out, Milly walked over to him and said, "You said you were going to take my boys Coogi?" The kid responded by saying he was just playing with me and we were going to leave it alone, but then he decided to mumble something. It was on from there.

He then flashed a knife, which now made us really think he was going to try and take the sweater. Maybe he was scared because of how we approached him, but his attitude and the knife didn't show fear. We beat on him from the high school until he ran next door to the Fire Department driveway. That day he learned not to play around or think of us as new freshman that he can just pick on. Not only did he learn it, everyone else learned it as well.

We would flip the freshman hazing rule around and turn it into the upperclassmen hazing. At times, I would come to school only to find that Matt and Otis would have an upperclassman between the lockers emptying his pockets. All I could do was laugh because I knew they weren't serious about it, but only doing it to send warning that we were not to be messed with. It didn't take long for everyone to figure out we were militant when it came to one another.

When it came to the basketball team, the only one of us that made it to play varsity ball our freshman year was Marcus and the rest of us wanted to be there. He had the opportunity to play with players such as Jon Paul (JP) Kobryn, Pedro (Pete) Cipriano, Carmine Charles, Quran (Kobe) Wimberly, Isaac (Zo) Ross, Donald (Don) Copeland, Dwayne (Dub) Lee, and Elijah (Eli) Ingram. All we could do is watch and cheer because as a group they were great players. We were good as well but just didn't make that varsity cut.

They walked around school with their heads up high as if nothing in the world was a bother to them. They had the girls, the in-school fans, the outside fans, and all the best clothing on Tag Days. The only one of us that shared that attention was Marcus. He was a part of their success 100% and we were trying to catch up and get there. No one would come early to watch the freshman and junior varsity basketball games. The gym only started to fill up when it was time for varsity to play.

We had respect for the varsity basketball players and at this time we would tend to follow in their footsteps. However, this was our freshman year when we were still wet behind the ears entering into the St. Anthony program. This probably would've been the only time we were set to follow the lead of the upperclassmen as Coach Hurley wished we did our junior year under the leadership of Terrence Roberts and Obie Nwadike. The only problem was, by our junior year we began to become more and more set in our own ways.

When the drama began to pick up with Matt, Beanie, their two girlfriends, and the downtown crew. We were quickly sidetracked from the positivity and the accomplishments the upperclassmen were set to experience. The fighting began and the upperclassmen acted as mediators. Isaac, who came from Marion Projects would always try to talk to us and stray us away from the nonsense. The others would call us wild and shake their heads after hearing about the fights we would get into.

We didn't notice then, but this is how we caught their attention and we took it the wrong way. We thought we were becoming one with these guys because we had their attention. Not seeing that they were shaking their heads at us in a sense of disgust. They would never verbally tell us they were disgusted with our behavior, but their body languages told it all. Yet, we seized the opportunity to become close. It was all we wanted from the beginning of our freshman year.

They tried to guide us without letting us know that's what they were trying to do. We would all hang out and have fun together. They introduced us to the girls and to the fun dice games we would sneak to play in the boy's bathroom. They tried their best to stray our minds away from the negativity, but it came to the point that it was too late.

Maybe it would have been simpler if they would have come straight out and said listen, you guys need to focus more on basketball. You need to squash whatever it is you have going on with these guys outside of school. That was too simple and we grew up in an era where everyone needed to be a tough guy. Showing any sign of weakness would result in you being the center of jokes every day in school. Everyone had a reputation to uphold. These guys were trying to tell us this without looking like punks in the eyes of our peers. However, we were too immature to figure out the signs.

As kids, it's amazing how much your peers and the people around you influence your life. When we were teenagers we cared too much about the unimportant things rather than what was really important. We cared about how we were viewed by our male friends and we definitely cared about how we looked in the eyes of the females. The females didn't like the nice guys that were quiet and couldn't defend them. They wanted a guy with swag, a guy that could dress, and a guy they could call on to handle their problems.

We weren't the only ones who had to uphold a reputation. We all did, even the upperclassmen. Thus leading to the reason they couldn't just come out and tell us to leave the drama alone. Even if they were bold enough to tell us that, we wouldn't have been able to take it to the next level and squash the problems. This would make us look weak in our opponent's eyes. With anything involving an opponent, when you notice their weakness, you attack it!

Going into our sophomore year we started to become more comfortable. We played basketball all summer with the varsity guys and we entered school knowing everybody especially the girls. The only thing was that we were still dealing with the outside drama. By this time, we were losing any chance of following the leadership of Elijah, Donald, and Dwayne, who were now seniors. Together these three guards were amazing. If one was having a bad game, no need to worry because the next one was stepping in. They were like mosquitoes in the summer time when you are outside at a barbecue. They just didn't go away.

At the start of the school year Coach Hurley would have White Eagle Hall opened up for us to have open gym basketball games. We would scrimmage against each other lining up from shortest to tallest, picking numbers one through five. We had a junior on the team and I can't quite remember his name, but he had problems. This kid would talk shit to all of us as if he was the best basketball player on earth. Truth be told, he couldn't play ball for shit. Obie and Terrence would abuse him in the paint. His attitude sucked and Eli, Don, and Dwayne would always tell him about it. He was a pain in the ass.

In school, this kid would talk so much shit it was ridiculous. He would talk shit and expect you not to say anything back to him. He thought he was a big time tough guy but we saw through him. In our eyes, he was softer than feathers. He had words with Lamar in school one day and ended up calling his cousin to meet him outside of White Eagle Hall after we finished open gym.

As we all were leaving White Eagle Hall, the kid's cousin approaches us and asks us why we were picking on his cousin. This kid was like the child that taunts his brother, but when the brother snaps back he runs and tells mommy. Well he ran and told his cousin. Before Lamar could get a word out to respond, I told his cousin off.

"Listen, your cousin is a big bitch and he called you down here for no reason! He can talk shit all day, but can't take it when it's dished back at him. So you must be a bitch as well for coming down here to defend your cousin that's six feet six inches tall, and has you by a whole foot! So he's a bitch and you're a bitch too!"

His cousin looks at me and responds, "Oh I'm a bitch right." As he finished asking his question he turns away from me and quickly swings his fist punching me in the side of my face. When he punched me it turned my head. By the time I turned my head back around to face him, Otis had punched him in the face and he fell on me. I then picked him up and slammed him. To the right of me, his cousin snuck up behind Lamar and punched him in the mouth, splitting the bottom part of his bottom lip.

We now found ourselves in a quick brawl. We all had jump ropes in our bags from open gym. Donald and Elijah took their jump ropes out and started to beat the kid's cousin with the jump ropes. Marcus punched the kid that sucker punched Lamar, knocking him to the ground. As a team, we all began to beat the kids up until they decided to retreat away.

This was probably the first and only time the upperclassman got into a brawl with us because this kid was just a straight up asshole. He wasn't a team player and it seemed like he was against everyone on the team for some reason. He didn't really last long at St. Anthony and ended up staying for one year if that.

Coach Gamble walked outside right after the confrontation. He asked us what was going on outside and what all the noise was about. We all acted like we were excited and was just having fun with each other. We responded by saying nothing Coach, we were all just goofing around. Then we walked off to catch the buses home.

During the summer, we would be in the gym three days a week working on our games and just playing basketball against each other. Dwayne lived exactly one block around the corner from me. Every so often I would hang out with him instead of being around the other guys I hung out with in the streets. As I think about it now, I realize how much hanging out with Dwayne kept me out of a lot of the trouble that was going on in other areas.

I would spend nights at his house playing video games and hanging out with Donald, Obie, Charles (Skee) Clark, who also played basketball at St. Anthony, and Antwan Thompson, another mutual friend. There was no drama hanging out with this crew. We would clown around and just do teenage things. No fights, guns, or anything of that sort. Simply teenagers having fun.

I recall a night I was supposed to hang out with them but instead I changed my mind and went to hang out with my friends on Dwight Street. One thing led to another and there was a big argument between some of the girls and guys on the block. My hand was in a splint because I hurt it playing basketball. I had a radio in the other hand and one of the girls was coming after me. As I was backing away from the girl, Donald, Dwayne, Antwan, and Thomas came riding by and saw me. They pulled over and told me to get in the car.

Instead of hanging out with them in the first place, I found myself in the middle of drama. It probably would have been worse if they didn't come because there was no telling what might have happened that night. This just goes to show the difference the upperclassmen made. Something as little as the people you hang around with, it changes the aspect of every situation you may come across.

Still when basketball season came the only one playing varsity ball was Marcus. There was no space for Otis, Beanie, and me on the team. The talents of the three guards were phenomenal and all other positions were locked. After our junior varsity games, we would stick around and watch the varsity team play. I have to be honest it was great watching the three guards play. They were tough and they all fed off of each other. The dribbling, ball movement, and execution of each play was all just so exciting to watch. To actually sit and watch Coach Hurley coach these guys was amazing.

At a certain point in our sophomore year we all kind of began to blend in with the seniors. Some of the trouble was slowing down and more of the time we found ourselves hanging in different places. We weren't hanging around in certain places because we were too busy trying to do the things Dwayne, Don, and Eli were doing. They were having fun, they weren't worried about drama and it was a good feeling.

They even began to watch our games and cheer us on. Coach Hurley would usually make the varsity team come early to the gym and we figured they watched our games because he made them. Otherwise, they would probably be hanging out until it was time for them to get ready. However, they watched, they cheered us on, and it felt good. Especially when I caught a dunk or two in the games and they went crazy.

We had become a family and at the time it wasn't as noticeable to me as it is now due to the difference in my maturity level. After the junior varsity season was over, I was moved up to the varsity team late in my sophomore year along with Otis, junior Thomas (T-Love) Hall, freshmen Derrick Mercer, and Barney Anderson.

As we all moved forward to share the glory of winning the State Championship and Tournament of Champions in the 2001-2002 season, Dwayne, Eli, and Don were set to leave for college. These were probably the only ones that could stray us away from any of the outside distractions and they were leaving. Towards the end of the school year they began to openly come out and tell us to calm down. Don especially would tell us but he came across in an overly aggressive way at times and we took it the wrong way maybe.

The seniors were leaving and it was our turn to step up for the next season. We were ready and we were confident. The confidence came from being around these guys and Coach Hurley. Before the season ended, Coach Hurley called a scrimmage day between our crew and the seniors. This was something we wanted to do so bad. They would constantly taunt us saying that we couldn't beat them and had no chance, but we told them we would be ready if the day ever came.

The competitive nature we all had was good motivation to all of us. We all wanted to win. You can play basketball and have fun playing it. Yet, if you don't have that drive to be competitive and want to win, what sense does it even make to play the sport? Coach Hurley would drive that competitiveness out of you and in this case, it trickled down.

In practice if the seniors were messing up, Coach Hurley would tell them that he had players on the junior varsity team that could come up and kick their asses for their spots. This would lead them to talk shit to us because Coach Hurley would get into their heads to motivate them. We already wanted to play against these guys just as a test to ourselves. So we got caught up in a back and forth debate at times with the guys and it was because we were so competitive.

I'm not sure if Coach Hurley heard about this, but when he called for the scrimmage we were all so damn excited. He gave us Marcus and Lamar so we could scrimmage five on five. Dwayne, Donald, Elijah, Obie, and Terrence against Marcus, Lamar, Otis, Beanie, and myself. We had a very good scrimmage and it was building our confidence even more because they actually weren't killing us on the court. We were getting pass their traps and their defense. We figured we couldn't run the St. Anthony plays because they would know every play so we implemented our Boys Club plays instead.

The scrimmage didn't end in a win/lose situation. Coach Hurley kept stopping the scrimmage. If there was an offensive play or defensive play that wasn't executed properly, Coach Hurley critiqued it. Still, this gave us confidence. There were certain parts of the scrimmage we were up a few points but all in all, it was great to get the opportunity to play against them. So as the seniors left, we felt we would bring two more State Championships and two more Tournament of Champions trophies in a row to the St. Anthony Program.

INTERVIEW VII

Q: Marcus. You were the only one to play varsity basketball as a freshman, how did that feel?

Marcus: *Playing varsity all four years, my first two years I was nervous. It was nerve wrecking. My first year I felt like there was so many expectations of me. It felt like if I didn't live up to them, I'm playing varsity for what. My sophomore year I felt like more was expected from me due to me already playing and being the CO-MVP for the State Championship my freshman year. To be recognized as a freshman, playing varsity for an elite team like St. Anthony High School. It was nerve wrecking and a great honor as well. There were only a select few in St. Anthony history that played varsity all four years. That was an honor.*

Q: As freshman, would you say we looked up to the upperclassmen? As far as the basketball team?

Beanie: *No, I don't think we looked up to them. I think they didn't really want to vibe with us anyway because they already had a bad taste in their mouths from us coming there. Coach Hurley used to tell them all the time, I got these freshmen coming in and they're coming in to take your spots. Automatically they looked at us as threats instead of all of us sticking together because we all played ball. St. Anthony was so small and we all could have come together and been a crew. They could have showed us how to deal with certain things when it came to Coach Hurley because they were already playing varsity. You would think by the time we got to varsity or Coach Hurley would have pulled us up our freshman year, we would have an understanding on how demanding he was or what he wanted. It was like they weren't big brothers to us. We were cool with them, but they weren't big brothers.*

Marcus: *Nah, we didn't. I didn't look up to none of them. We all came in there with chips on our shoulders. I respected some of them as far as basketball was concerned, but as individuals I didn't look up to them. From where I grew up, you don't show respect unless it's earned. I didn't know none of them, I wasn't raised around none of them. You have to earn respect at the end of the day.*

Otis: *I wouldn't say we looked up to them. I would say we respected them. We didn't look up to no other players besides ourselves. We felt like they couldn't beat us if we played a five on five no matter what Coach Hurley said or what the paper said. Nobody could beat us five on five. I wouldn't say we looked up to them. I would say we respected them and they gave us the same respect as well. So it was mutual.*

Q: What do you think strayed us away from taking after the guys like Elijah Ingram, Donald Copeland, and Dwayne Lee?

Beanie: *We wanted to make our own impression. We wanted our own image. Go out with our own bang. Not to be mimicking anybody else.*

Marcus: *We were different. They weren't into the streets and they didn't run around in the same areas we ran around in. It was different environments with them. The way we came up was totally different. He wanted us to follow their footsteps but we were a complete different breed from what he was used to. We were doing shit that nobody was even thinking about. We got to St. Anthony, the upperclassmen looked at us like, y'all motherfuckers are wild! Telling us we can't do this or do that. We looked at them like they are crazy. We going to do what we want to do. That's just how we were. We wanted to be ourselves.*

Otis: *I think it was more of the fact that we didn't want to give into Coach Hurley or give into what people wanted us to do. We could have separated, went our separate ways, and just did what they wanted us to do. We didn't though. We didn't. We just weren't changing for nobody. I think that's what made it better in the end because we stuck to what we knew and it worked out.*

Q: I know we all had our moments when we hung out with those guys; Do you think hanging out with them kept us out of some of the other trouble we were getting into?

Beanie: *Yeah, most definitely. Most definitely. Some of them grew up around our areas, but they weren't moving around how we were moving around. Not for nothing, we liked to hang out sometimes and they really wouldn't hang out. So it's like we are all a crew. Think about it. Everybody in different areas, one person hangs*

here, one person hangs there, one person hangs there. Then it's like alright we are going to get cool with everybody's crew. If I'm with him, I'm going to be in the area where he hangs at and if I'm with him, I'm going to be in the area he hangs out at. So we were all amongst each other like one big family. They never moved around like us. Of course hanging with them would keep us out of trouble.
Marcus: *Yeah, with me I hung with them a little more. It was a different environment. When you hang with different people it ain't the same. It just depends on the people you hang with. Hanging out with them we were in a complete different atmosphere. I can't even describe the shit they were doing, but we were just different.*
Otis: *Yeah, it was different. The people we used to hang around were friends from the neighborhood. I think they knew how to separate the streets and it didn't affect them as much as it affected us. We would come to school like, man I got jumped or whatever. Moms pissed me the fuck off and I want to move. Ask mommy if I can come stay there. All types of shit. They just focused on ball. Hanging around them was different.*

Q: When Coach Hurley moved those of us that weren't on varsity up to the varsity team our sophomore year, how did that feel? How did it feel to be able to experience winning a State Championship and Tournament of Champions Title?
Otis: *It made me feel like I wanted to win some more. I want to be a part of the reason we win. I want to be the reason we win. I want us to have our own legacy within the school like the people before us. If we wouldn't have won, it just would have been easy for them to say, man I told you they were fucked up. They were knuckleheads. I knew this was going to happen. By senior year it all started sinking in. I began to change. I wanted to go to college. I knew I had a chance to play. A chance to go to college for free. To get away from Jersey City.*

ARRIVAL OF SEAN MCCURDY

Sean McCurdy!!!

Every time I think of that name I think of the "Great White Hope." It seemed as if he was GOD'S gift to earth when he arrived at St. Anthony. Maybe he was but we didn't see it. When he arrived, we welcomed him with open arms, but this was off the court. We didn't expect him to come anywhere close to getting in the rotation until he got some time in. Shitting me if we weren't in for a big time rude awakening.

Sean came into school and he was cool, but our crew felt there was something strange about him. It seemed like he had a hidden agenda and we picked up a sneaky vibe from him. He had a hidden agenda alright because Sean wasn't coming into the school to make friends; he was coming there strictly to play basketball. This was a business move, sort of like "Insider Trading." He knew Coach Hurley's name was good enough to get him anywhere and he traded in the bad stock for the good. All he needed was to get his foot in the door and he would make it happen, and he did.

Sean came to a few open gyms to play basketball with us and we really didn't expect this kid from Connecticut to come so far to attend St. Anthony High School. Surprise hit us when we saw him in school with the uniform on and we knew things would now change. We didn't believe he would get too much playing time; he hadn't even been around for the past two years. So we paid him no mind and openly welcomed him. Slowly but surely, we began to notice that things were changing and it kind of broke our focus. Well, the little focus that we had.

This was a rich kid coming from Connecticut every day, he would be scared straight out of Jersey City, we all thought. However, Sean wasn't going to be living in the areas of Jersey City we lived in. He would be living in the high rises on the water front behind Newport Mall. Famous actors lived in those places. He wasn't going to have to worry about coming to our part of town or running into the same drama and bullshit that we did.

Sean was going to be put in the rotation and Sean was definitely going to play. He could dribble the ball, he could shoot, he had good moves, and he had a motive. He wanted desperately to get to the next level. He wanted it more than any of us did. The difference with him was that he could focus on just doing what he had to do in school and basketball, but we couldn't. Our focus was on the problems we had outside the gym, then basketball, and Coach Hurley. He could give it 100% and we could not. He already had an advantage.

We all thought of Sean as a good player but just not good enough to play over any of us. He could play but if you put pressure on him, his game was out of the window. Foul him hard and it would excite him. He would get so excited that his excitement forced him to make mistakes. We all knew this and when we played against players that were rough and in your grill type of players, they would pick up on it as well. None of this would stop Sean's hunger, or his mother Cindy's hunger.

We were getting annoyed with the presence of Sean. It really put us over edge when he walked into the gym and Coach Hurley called him something like a breath of fresh air. Why did he say that? Otis, Marcus, Beanie, Lamar, and I were livid. This rich kid who just came to our school was being treated like royalty. It wasn't at all because he was white; shit color didn't matter to us at all. It didn't matter if he was purple, pink, red, or fucking green, this kid had to go.

We all knew Coach Hurley thought of us as the biggest knuckleheads and screw ups ever in the history of the St. Anthony basketball program.

Now Sean was here, who wasn't a knucklehead like we were. He wasn't dealing with the nonsense we were dealing with. Sean was more focused than any of us would or could ever be. So we had to come up with a game plan to get into his head. We decided to toughen him up just a little, or maybe I should say a lot.

When practice broke way and Sean would get the ball, he was a target to all of us. We all had a clear vision set on Sean to hit him with the hardest fouls ever. It was sort of like Bobby Boucher from the movie "Water Boy," and how he was with his water. If anyone said anything negative about water he would attack, and if anyone said anything positive about Sean, we would attack. We fouled him hard and had no remorse at all.

If Sean went up for a layup he was hit hard and tossed to the floor. As he would get up he probably got a knee to the head or pushed back down by "accident." While he would dribble, he got hand checked and stiff armed. If he had a fast break he would be grabbed and pulled back. If he was running up the court and not paying attention, he would get a surprise shoulder to the chest. We would basically beat this kid up on the court without balling up a fist.

Eventually it got to the point that is was noticeable. Coach Hurley stopped practice one day. "What the fuck is going on here? Is there some type of a problem with Sean? If anyone purposely fouls Sean again there is going to be problems!" From there the fouling was over. Sean had gotten lucky. We were so much in the zone that we had reached the point of fouling him even when he was nowhere near the ball.

It was starting to sink in. Sean was here to stay and he was going to be a major factor in the rest of our St. Anthony careers. His mother's friend Greg Bracey would eventually become our strength and conditioning trainer. This kid was becoming a cancer to us. Sean, his mother, and now her friend were all making a move into the St. Anthony program. It seemed as if he had it out for us.

We all took it very hard and it was not at all anything in particular with Sean. It was simply because he hadn't been there the two years prior dealing with all the bullshit we had to deal with.

Coaches imitating Coach Hurley and yelling at us.

Teachers threatening us, telling us if we didn't get our acts together they would tell Coach Hurley on us!

The summer time open gyms and all the hard work we put in!

All of the camps we went to just to better our skills and be prepared to play together our junior year in high school.

Coach Hurley constantly on our backs about how we didn't contribute shit to the previous two years of Tournament of Champions. How much we were knuckleheads and the worst bunch of kids he ever encountered.

Sean wasn't around for any of the fighting or bullshit in the streets we had to deal with growing up in Jersey City.

He was an outsider and his life was easy. He would never know what it felt like to go home from practice and fear for his life. He would never know what it felt like to get to the corner of his block and have a gun pointed to his head because someone wanted to rob him of his valuables. He would never know! He would never know! He would never know!

It felt like we were robbed of our previous years of hard work and I still say today that Otis Campbell took it the hardest. Remember, this went all the way back to elementary school with Otis and I. Mr. Broncado telling Otis that he wouldn't last at St. Anthony High School under Coach Hurley's rules. Otis was upset. Even worse than upset, Otis was hurt.

Sean's presence was destroying our chemistry. We were beginning to lose the love we had for basketball. The streets were against us, the teachers were against us, and Coach Hurley was against us. It seemed like everything and everyone was against us. Otis didn't want to play anymore so he decided to bring in his uniform and hand it to Sister Alan. Everything he had worked for was handed to Sean. Sean played good in just a few open gyms, did well in a few practices, and seemed like he was just handed a spot.

Coach Hurley had his way of playing mind games and I was always on Otis about how the things that Coach would tell us didn't matter. "He just wants us to work harder Otis, that's it. If we work harder things will change." I didn't believe shit I was telling Otis because I actually didn't know what to believe. All I knew was that I didn't want him to leave the team. Otis looked at me and said, "Shelt, he doesn't like us. All he does is tell us we are a bunch of knuckleheads and the worst group of kids he ever had. Sean wasn't here for none of this shit we went through and he just comes here and gets a spot! He ain't go through what the fuck we went through." Otis was right, and we were falling apart as a team.

I didn't believe that Coach Hurley didn't like us, yet it was the mind games that confused us all. The mind games had gotten to Otis and he went through a moment where his mind wasn't working hard enough to put the king in checkmate. Otis eventually came back to the team but he wasn't 100% the same, there was still built up anger and animosity in him.

The first season Sean played with us was our junior year. Obie Nwadike and Terence Roberts were seniors and the leaders of the team. We didn't know how or if they even felt any way about Sean's presence, but at the same time they weren't as outspoken about it as we were. Compared to our group, Obie and Terence were like obedient puppies. If the dog owner turned their head, they would still listen to the last command the owner told them. Our crew on the other hand, was completely different. If the dog owner turned his/her head, who knows what the hell we would get into.

However, Obie and Terence had nothing to worry about. They were seniors and nothing was getting in their way. They had no reason to feel the way we did about Sean because this was their last year. They weren't negatively viewed in Coach Hurley's eyes like we were. They had their college scholarships already prepared on golden platters. Sean was only a threat to us.

Sean became close to Derrick Mercer and Barney Anderson who were in the same grade level as he was. It didn't bother either one of them if Sean played or not. Sean played a different position than both of them, which meant it wasn't going to be any of their playing time that was compromised. Otis could play anywhere from the two to the four positions, as could Lamar, Marcus, and I. However, Otis had the better jump shot out of us all, so the two-guard position would fit him the best.

This is where the disruption came when Sean arrived. If Sean never came to St. Anthony this would be a battle between the crew. We could care less which one of us was playing, as long as the time was shared between us. We felt we worked hard for it. Shit, even if it was Derrick, Barney, or anyone else he was playing over, we still took it personally. If they were too blind to see that this kid was given free lunch and we had to pay for it, that was on them.

It's not like it was only one of us that felt this way about Sean, it was the entire crew. Coach Hurley embedded the importance of hard work in our heads. He instilled hard work and the fact that if you worked hard you would play, but you had to work for it. Now being that we had this entrenched in our minds, we thought to ourselves, where the hell is Sean's hard work?

It felt like one side of us was listening to Coach Hurley's hard work theory. Yet the other side was saying, well if you just transfer and can play ball you don't have to work hard for it. Either way it was work on top of work. All of this took away our hunger to continue to work hard at basketball our junior year.

Off the court, it was like a completely different world. In school, we would talk to Sean and sometimes hang out. It was very weird. We didn't feel quite the same way about him as we did when we were in the gym. At the end of the day, it wasn't like we didn't like him. It was just the mere fact that everything was given to him. Why couldn't we be fed off of the golden spoon? Why did we have to work so hard for time on the basketball court? Yet, Sean walks in and gets the green light from the very start.

Outsiders would always say it came down to one thing, it's sad to say but they thought it was the color of his skin. He was the only white player on a team full of black players. From our point of view, Sean wasn't a color. We weren't worried about black or white or whatever the case may have been. We had white friends that played basketball with us at the Boys & Girls Club. We had white friends in elementary school and in high school.

We hated to hear anything about Sean being white because it wasn't that at all. If someone asked us a question about how we felt about Sean being white, we would stop them dead in the middle of their question. This was something that would force us to let our guards down a little when it came to Sean. We didn't like the things we were hearing from outsiders. Someone was always trying to stir up drama. We felt like things were handed to Sean, but not because he was white.

Cindy McCurdy!!!

Boy was she an exciting woman. Our nickname for her was "Cruella de Vil," because we felt she was a vicious character. She was out for blood. Everything was about Sean and Michael. Michael was Sean's older brother who played basketball and she felt he didn't get his fair chance to attend a Division I basketball program. She felt this way because of the program he played for back in Connecticut and she wasn't going to allow the same thing to happen with Sean.

Cindy was a piece of work. At the games or in the parking lots, it seemed like her mouth never closed. She said whatever it was she felt like saying, to whomever, and whenever. We didn't know her son Michael at all but it seemed like we did because she spoke about him to the point it felt like he was around us all the time. With Cindy, came her friend Greg.

Like said previously, Greg became our strength and conditioning trainer. He was alright I guess, but we felt he was only there for his own motives.

It was like they all swindled their ways into the program, deep into the program at that. Sean on the team getting plenty of playing time, his mom getting what she wanted, but what did Greg want. They all wanted something and we were convinced. Greg was an African American male with long dreadlocks in his hair and to us we found the relationship weird. Sean's mother was full of excitement and loud, but Greg was laid back and a smooth talker. The two didn't seem to mix.

There was a time we had a game in Neptune, New Jersey. Sean's mother was in the stands going off. We heard her clear across the gym screaming. Apparently, words were exchanged between her and some parents from Neptune that were sitting right beside her. Now this was on the verge to becoming a riot. Neptune, New Jersey was not known to be one of the best parts of New Jersey. It wasn't quite clear if Cindy knew that at the time, but she would find out this day. From the bench, we saw one of the mothers jump up in her face. Behind Sean's mother were the other fans, friends, and family from Neptune.

We looked down the bench and Coach Hurley didn't seem to notice this, but Greg did. The game was on the verge to being stopped and Greg leaped up to rush over to defuse the situation. Mumbling under his breath, when he got in the stands he separated Cindy from the crowd. She was still going off and the Neptune fans weren't backing down either. Whatever happened, both parties were ticked off. For the rest of the game Greg couldn't do anything but shake his head.

We would tease at Greg and he was probably the only one from the coaching staff that we could pull this off with, along with Coach Darren Erman. These were probably the only two we felt we could actually talk to about things and they would give us feedback without judging us. "Greg, what are you doing with Sean's mom? What are you in it for?" We would ask. A blank stare and a response of, "Come on man, do the workouts," followed with a laugh. We all figured he was in it for something, but he definitely wouldn't tell us if he was. Why would he? Shit, we were only teenagers, we were just kids.

Greg had us hitting the weights, working out, and conditioning. He took his role very seriously and he was going to make sure that we were strong and fit. He looked like he was all muscle and didn't have one bit of fat on his body. As we worked out he would watch every move we made. When we started slacking, his favorite words would pop out, "Come on mannnn, do the workouts!" As he always dragged the letter N at the end of man.

One-day Derrick (Boo) Mercer and Barney Anderson were clowning around. Greg was becoming furious. He said his favorite line a few times but they weren't listening. The next thing you know he snapped. He jumped in the air and did a side kick at Boo, just missing him. He looked like Bruce Lee in an old Bruce Lee film when he would hit you with one of those deadly sidekicks to the chest.

"DO THE WORKOUTS MAN, JUST DO THE WORKOUTS!!!"

We all tightened up and Boo looked scared as shit, it was so funny. He missed Boo and I don't think he was even trying to really kick him but more scare him. Boo moved and fell over the bench. We laughed to ourselves when Greg turned his head. We all whispered to each other, "If that was one of us and he kicked at us our reaction probably wouldn't have been good." The turnout would have probably been different. We were all fighters and Greg would have got himself punched in the face throwing a fake kick at one of us. Not only punched in the face we all probably would have jumped on his ass and worried about explaining it to Coach Hurley later.

We began to clown Boo as the workouts continued. This made Greg even more upset because the clowning around was interrupting the workouts. We had finally pushed him to his limit. He turned to the one thing that all the teachers, assistant coaches, and everyone else would turn to, threatening us with telling Coach Hurley. We didn't respect those who did that, it was annoying. No one seemed to be able to hold their own weight.

Greg didn't like the fact that Coach Hurley had that type of control over us, as we frustrated him more and more it would slip out of his mouth. "Y'all rather listen to the other man right! Y'all only listen to Coach Hurley right! What he got that I don't got? Oh yeah!" As he pointed to the sideline, implementing that Coach Hurley had the power to make sure that's where we sat during the games if we acted up.

When our senior year came around we began to warm up to Sean. It finally smacked us in the face that this was our team and this year was it. We had to win everything and Sean was going to be right by our sides regardless. We were used to him by now and Cindy's exciting behavior had become part of the norm. However, there were still things we didn't know about Cindy. It came to us by surprise when we heard a rumor that she invited herself to Duke's Head Coach, Mike Krzyewski's office one year to introduce him to her son Michael. When she found out he wasn't there, she then wrote a letter to him. We thought to ourselves, wow! Now that puts the icing on the cake. It damn sure was a funny story, and of course we put our own little spin to the story. Yet, this was the life of the adventurous McCurdy family, full of surprises.

INTERVIEW VIII

Q: What did you guys think about Sean when he first came to St. Anthony?

Beanie: *I didn't care for him. I'm going to be honest with you. Coach Hurley made it that way because he brought him in and it was just like, we been here already. Coach brought him in and it was like he was the Golden Child. He was GOD! He didn't even put work in yet. We've been putting work in since eighth-grade when we went to Coach Hurley's camp in the Poconos. It was just as if he praised this kid as soon as he came. So at first I didn't care for Sean.*

Marcus: *Well it's crazy because we went to camp and Sean was on my team at Poconos camp. Me and him were playing and he kept asking me about St. Anthony. He's from Connecticut and he kept asking me about St. Anthony, St. Anthony, St. Anthony. After the camp was over, next thing you know I see the kid at White Eagle Hall. Like, what the fuck you doing here? When he first came I didn't expect nothing of it, but it kind of got funny once he came to the school. It was weird after that. A lot of shit started changing. You started to notice a lot of things. When he first came it was cool but after a while, you looked at shit differently.*

Otis: *I thought they laid out the red carpet for him because he could shoot. I guess that was Hurley's way of teaching me a lesson, not giving me a spot. I got to earn it. But I felt like I earned it. I felt like I earned it all through the years. I didn't just come to the program and now I'm the Golden Child. Now I just get thrown into a position. I can't lie though, Sean worked his ass off. He was a hard worker. Us playing with him, I had a change of mind about him. He worked for it and ended up deserving everything that happened. I didn't mind playing with him at all after that. It ended up working out.*

Q: Did you guys feel like the importance of hard work Coach Hurley always talked about was thrown out the window when Sean came?

Beanie: *Yeah. It was definitely thrown out of the window because it was like, we were working hard for what. You just let him come in and pretty much do* *whatever he wanted at first. You let him do whatever he wanted until you realized, okay, he ain't turning out to be what you thought he was going to be or whatever it was that happened. Then he started getting yelled at a little bit. Still at first, it was like Coach Hurley just handed him a plate of food like, here, have it.*

Marcus: *Nah, not really. But it seemed like there was some type of favoritism. I don't know what it was. Maybe because he was white, because he was the only white kid on the team. I don't know if it was that, I don't know if it was because he had money. I always felt Coach Hurley was harder on us because we were city kids. He probably felt he had to be tougher on us. Sean was like a baby. You say something to him, he starts pouting, getting frustrated. He couldn't handle the yelling and screaming like we could. It felt like he was hard on us all around. When it came to Sean, the attitude was different.*

Otis: *To be honest, I really didn't feel too bad because I knew I could play. It didn't bother me much. I wasn't worried about it. I felt, it is what it is. I was upset when it first went down. Yeah! I just didn't feel like he put in as much work as we did to get there. He just got there.*

Q: How exciting was Sean's mother Cindy?

Beanie: *Ohhhh.* **(Laughing) (Grabs Face)** *Ms. McCurdy!* **(Laughing)** *Whoooaaa! Remember the Neptune game! What happened? A kid from Neptune fouled Sean or something happened, I don't know. She was going off.* **(Laughing)**

Marcus: (Laughing) *She was happy man. She was too happy. She was a great woman. I respected her. She was all about the team and about the guys. She came with a lot of energy. She was a great person.*

Otis: *She was just so involved. She was too involved. She could be like a nag sometimes. Let Sean play, let him be a man. Let him get roughed up. This not Connecticut! Shit different over here. But she also loved the team as well. At the same time, there wasn't anything that she wouldn't do for us. It played itself out to be a good situation to be honest. I liked her a lot. I liked Greg too.*

Q: How about this one, "Come on Mannnn, Do the workouts"?
Beanie: (Laughing) *He threw that kick that time! He was like I could have killed you with that kick.* **(Laughing)** *If I wanted to.* **(Laughing)**
Marcus: *That guy!* **(Laughing)** *I don't even know if he helped or not. He tried to do his best. I just don't know if it helped us.*
Otis: (Laughing) (Imitating Greg's Voice) *"Come on Boo! Kick you in your fucking face Mannn! Don't ever disrespect me like that Mannn!"* **(Laughing) (Imitating Greg's Voice)** *"Come on baby, you know how I am Mannn."*

I kind of feel like once our senior year came around we began to warm up to Sean and stop worrying about him so much. I think our focus shifted on winning everything and going undefeated.
Q: Would you guys agree?
Beanie: *I agree with that. But then again, the way Coach Hurley portrayed Sean, made us look at Sean differently. Then we started to get to know him. So it was different senior year. Sean, Coach Hurley made him that way. When we got to know Sean, it was alright, we were comfortable with Sean. Plus, we were trying to win. We didn't want to hear that shit! The talk about us leaving without a championship! That's a negative. We all going to get cool, we going to win this championship. That's going to be that and then we are going down in history. Simple!*
Marcus: *It did. After we lost our junior year we distinguished that we weren't going to lose next year or go through that same feeling. We lost by fucking four points. We knew we shouldn't have lost. We said we weren't going to lose senior year and stuck by it. The whole summer we were grinding. From that loss, we never lost again.*

THE TEAM 2002-2003: JUNIOR YEAR

FOUR, FOUR, FOUR, FOUR.

Four was the bad luck number this year. This was the year we lost every game by four. Four regular season games, four points each game, and four points to St. Pat's to move forward to the final four to compete in the Boys Parochial B Championship. We lost every damn game by four sleazy points. We had a rough season this year and I especially lost my interest in playing basketball any longer.

For some reason, this year we were all over the place with injuries and just so many other things. This was Sean's first season playing with us and we had to adapt to him coming in and being in the rotation. Some guys were accepting of him while others weren't. We all waited our time and him coming into the school kind of threw a wrench in everything. Morale was down from the start with that transition and we had to help each other stay confident.

With Sean, injuries, and all the other distractions, it had already seemed like this season was doomed from the beginning. Still from my point of view, Otis was bothered the most from the situation. I mean we all felt we worked so hard and waited our turns, but Otis didn't get over it as easy as the rest of us. We complained and bitched to each other, but it didn't mean shit. He was a good player, but in our eyes he shit the bed when we played against tough opponents. We figured this would expose him and he would be out of the picture.

Otis was at a point he didn't want to play anymore and I believe he wanted to quit the team at some point. His behavior changed, his view towards the team changed, and I can't single him out because all of our views changed. Yet, we kind of stuck it out and figured out a way to come together in order to uplift each other.

We lost our first home game in two years this season which was to Life Center Academy of Burlington with a low scoring game of 48-44. The two years prior to that, the varsity team lost to St. Raymond from the Bronx. At halftime of the Life Center game, we were down by one and we ended the game making only four out of fifteen free throws. With two losses, we had already lost more games this year than the team the previous year with a 29-1 record. They ended their season as State Champions and Tournament of Champions. Things just weren't looking golden for us at all and maybe it was just GOD's plan to prepare us for the next year.

Everyone in the rotation this year on any given day could give you double figures. It was just the matter of what type of game you were having and how at ease your nerves were. Terrence and Obie hands down would be the team leaders this year. Terrence standing at about six feet eight inches tall, bullied everyone in the paint and Obie was as strong as a tank. This year everything was about these two and it was very well deserved. However, if they weren't having their best games then they definitely had back up.

Terrence and Obie both shared double figures as the team leaders and mostly all other points were distributed between the rest of us players. After receiving our second loss early on to Life Center, we began to go on a winning streak. Redeeming ourselves with a win against Christian Brothers Academy (CBA) with a score of 41-29, Obie scoring 17 points and Terrence 14 points. Winning a game after a loss is always good because you get that spark of confidence back that is very well needed. Especially after losing and then getting screamed at by Coach Hurley.

As we won our next two games we were headed out to North Carolina to play in a Hoop Group's Challenge Series at Duke's Cameron Indoor

Stadium. We played against Hopkins of Minnesota who was ranked number 13 in the nation. They also had Kris Humphries on their team who was on his way to Duke and eventually drafted into the NBA. This was Sean's first game playing with us because he had to sit out for a knee injury.

We ended up winning the game 63-46 and for the first time this season having four players scoring double figures. Terrence 14 points, Beanie 13 points, Obie 12 points, and Sean with 10 points in his opening St. Anthony basketball game. Kris Humphries had game high with 17 points and 9 of the 17 was in the fourth quarter when we winded down all the pressure. So we'll just say he really only contributed 8 points.

Our winning streak continued and we were becoming a team that looked like we were on the verge of having a three-peat of State Championships and Tournament of Champions. Our team leaders were doing well at leading the team on the court and everyone was contributing. Suddenly, what I call a "misfortunate fortune" took place. Obie injured his ankle and had to take time healing.

Now this was unfortunate for Obie who was doing very well along with Terrence in leading the team and contributing important points to our wins. Yet, his misfortune became a fortunate situation for me. Coach Hurley felt I was working hard enough and could fill the void in Obie's absence. He granted me the opportunity to start while Obie took his time to heal. I was very excited. One, because I was getting a chance to prove myself, and two because Coach Hurley had enough confidence in me to give me the opportunity.

I knew I could get the job done and was confident enough that I wouldn't let the team or Coach Hurley down. With Obie's absence, it put a spark in several of us and honestly we all began to step up. Marcus, Lamar, and myself proved that we could all put the ball in the basket. Though we all stepped up, I tried to go the extra mile so that I wouldn't lose that starting spot. Even if Obie returned I still wanted to try my hardest to either keep the spot or lock in more playing time.

Things started off very well I could say and with Obie not playing I think I was averaging about nine points plus a game. We topped St. Josephs Metuchen with a score of 75-53 and Morris Catholic 65-44. In the games I started in, I was playing well and my confidence level was increasing. When we were set to play against Linden High School this was my third game starting and I scored my high of 14 points. Things couldn't possibly get any worst, only better from here.

As Obie began to heal and get himself back into the rotation he still wasn't fully where he needed to be with his ankle. I would still start the games in his place and greedily I hoped his healing process took as long as possible. I was loving the playing time and becoming more and more focused. I'm quite sure we were all loving the extra playing minutes and points. With Obie out, our names were in the Star Ledger more, we were being interviewed, and everyone was proving that they could contribute.

Everything was coming along and we were set to play against Lincoln High School from Brooklyn, whose star player was Sebastian Telfair. Sebastian was highly spoken about and rumors were that he was going straight to the NBA from high school. We stayed at a hotel close to the Sovereign Bank Arena in Trenton, where we would be one of four teams playing in the Arena. One of the other teams was Lebron James's St. Vincent-St. Mary team who was playing against Westchester, CA.

Prior to heading to Trenton, we were all excited and very anxious. We considered ourselves one of the best teams in the nation and we weren't about to go to Trenton just to let Telfair have his way with us. We knew we were going to a tournament that had two players going to the NBA straight from high school, but this was St. Anthony. To hell with any other team that was going to be playing in that arena that weekend. We wanted everyone to know that the St. Anthony team meant business like always.

With two highly ranked players such as Sebastian Telfair and Lebron James, we knew that big time college coaches and NBA Scouts would be lurking in the stands. I was so excited and doing everything to prepare for this game. I just knew if I had the game of a life time I would put myself in a position to be looked at by a big-time college. Still, Obie was not fully himself and at this point he became frustrated because his ankle was still bothering him. He had a pep talk with me before we went to Trenton telling me to do my thing and play hard.

With all of the excitement and anxiousness leading up to the Lincoln game, we got bad news that Coach Hurley's mom was very sick. This lead to Coach Hurley not being able to come to the game so he could spend time with his mom and family. We all felt very bad about the situation and playing against a team like this, we selfishly wanted Coach Hurley to be there. Yet, we all very well understood his reason why he couldn't make it. Nervousness began to kick in, but we were still very confident in ourselves that we would pull through without him.

At this point, our goal went from going out to Trenton to make sure we won and impress college coaches, to going out there to win for Coach Hurley and his mom. When we got to the hotel we had already planned on putting our things away and getting right out of the rooms to try to meet up with Sebastian and Lebron. We wanted to know what kind of guys these were and to also talk some shit about the upcoming games.

As we got to the hotel and went to check in, there was just a very pleasant vibe floating around. Everything just seemed too pleasant and it was weird. We got in the elevators to go up to our rooms and as the elevators stopped on the floors below our room floor, there were different girls on every floor just smiling. As they smiled they leaned over looking into the elevators, and we would hear them saying, "I think Lebron is in that elevator." Boy, oh boy we knew we needed to meet up with Lebron and we were going to have some fun this night.

Unfortunately, our fun was cut very short. Coach Gamble told us once we got into our rooms, not to come out. Man, how pissed we were. It wasn't even late and we were stuck in our rooms while all the fun seemed to be waiting outside. So of course, we all planned to sneak out of the rooms and get to all the festivities. We called each other's rooms trying to come up with the best plan and we thought we had it all figured out. Still the coaches were a step ahead of us.

We opened the door to look into the hallways and the coaches were sitting outside of the rooms. They really just screwed up any chance of us having fun. Hoping that they got tired and went into their rooms, we constantly checked the peepholes every so often, but they didn't leave. We eventually tired out and just went to sleep. There went our chances of hanging with Lebron and Sebastian. Now it was just back to business.

When we got into the Arena we all were very hyped up and still anxious. We couldn't stop saying, "We bringing this one back for Coach Hurley and his family!" Coach Hurley always taught us to work up a sweat and get loose during warmups, so we all went extra hard in the layup lines. Doing air dunks because you couldn't touch the rim or it would be a technical foul before the game even started. I had the highest vertical jump on the team at the time and could jump out of the gym. All I could think of was how I wanted to dunk on Sebastian in front of everyone.

The game kicked off and I got to an early start. They jumped on us with a 4-0 lead, but I was hot. Two layups, a spin move fade away jump shot that landed me on high school sports weekly, and fouled on the way to the basket, and-one. I was in my zone, playing solid defense and everything was going our way. I never had this feeling playing for the St. Anthony program ever, that unstoppable feeling.

As I'm shooting my and-one free throw at the foul line, swish it goes in. Sebastian runs by me and punches me in my stomach as he whispers, "Slow it down," but I had no intentions on slowing down one bit. Phased a little by the sneak shot to the stomach I quickly got over it and got back on defense. My adrenaline was high and I was so into the game that nothing could possibly stop me. With zero fouls, solid defense, and doing everything well on the offensive end, the next thing you know I get subbed out the game.

As I'm running to the bench a million questions are literally running through my mind.

"Did I do something wrong? Why is he taking me out? Do I look tired or something? Does he not see that I'm hot right now? Is he trying to lose the game or something? Would Coach Hurley have taken me out right now? What the hell is going on here?"

I get to the bench and everyone on the bench is saying the same thing. Obie says, "Ice I don't know why he took you out man, you are balling right now," and I responded by saying I was thinking the same thing. At this point I'm getting frustrated because it was the first quarter, I already had nine points, I was hot, and had so much more energy to keep playing with the same intensity. As the first quarter ended and second quarter began I was still on the bench. No one was stopping me when I was on the court, no one.

When Coach Gamble finally put me back in, I believe it was close to the very end of the second quarter. At this point I was pissed because something wasn't right. I began to believe Coach Gamble was trying to jeopardize the game or just had something against me or something. Sebastian ended the first half with only six points and everything was going well. Even though we led by just a few points ending the first half, I felt that if I had stayed in we would be leading by double digits and if not double digits, close to it.

Things took a turn in the second half and everything just started falling apart. Sebastian seemed to be getting every foul call and my hot streak was just taken over by frustration as well as having a million other thoughts going through my mind. Obie was playing and you could tell he was still hurting from the ankle pain. He couldn't even run up and down the court without limping and making painful faces. What the hell had just happened?

We ended up losing the game by four points with a score of 65-61 and Sebastian who had only six points in the first half ended the game with 26 points. We shook hands in the end and Sebastian says, "I'm glad he took you out the game," as he smiled and shook his head. I was furious and you could probably see steam rushing from the top of my head. When we got into the locker room, Coach Gamble began to scold me about a play that he drew up and me not being in the exact spot or something of that sort. Yet, all I could think about was the fact that we lost and we weren't bringing the win back home for Coach Hurley and his family. Also, the fact that he may have messed up any chances I had to be looked at by college coaches.

I was dreading getting back to the gym with Coach Hurley because I didn't know where things would go and I felt we disappointed him. His mom passed away and what would have been better than the next time he saw us was bringing home a win against Sebastian Telfair. I knew the mistake that Coach Gamble said I made would get back to him; even though I felt we had no chance of getting the lead back at that point. The question was, what was going to happen next?

Sure enough, Coach Hurley got on my case and told me that I wouldn't have to worry about playing as much once Obie got back from his injury. Just like that I was in the doghouse. From there my confidence was shot, my hunger and love for the game felt like it was taken away from me. At this point my frustration was not with Coach Hurley, but I felt Coach Gamble did so many things wrong. It reminded me of that summer league game when Coach Gamble told Thomas to go trap the ball and my frustration towards him increased. I was torn and that love I always had for the game had begun to slowly dissipate.

The loss to Lincoln ended a 12-game winning streak and it was our third loss of the season. Our next loss came shortly after to Camden Catholic, 52-48. Again, losing by four points. Obie's ankle was still not back to normal and we were just a few games away from the state tournament. To add fuel to the fire, Beanie ended up being suspended from the team. All around things weren't looking well at all.

Our first game in the North Parochial B tournament against Montclair-Kimberley was a walk in the park beating them by 40 points, 74-34. It was the next game against St. Patrick's that we would have to be prepared for. This game we needed to have our A-games and nothing less. Mike Nardi, Robert Hines, and the rest of the St. Patrick's crew were in full force. We were down Beanie and Obie's ankle was still not at 100%.

With all the obstacles in the world in front of us, we still were very confident that we could pull this off. One thing we was sure about, was that the winner of this game would be the ones to win the State Championship and the Tournament of Champions. I was getting somewhat back into my grove after I had a good game against Montclair-Kimberley scoring 12 points and was sure I could redeem myself completely against St. Patrick's. The big games always motivated me and once again I was at a point where I was hyped up.

We played the game at St. Peter's College, which to remind you is my father's alma mater, and the gym was packed. We were ready, I was ready. Warm ups were going well; Obie was going to play but we were still down Beanie. Although he was off the team, as we glanced into the crowd Beanie still showed his presence. With Beanie, things would have definitely made a difference but we were prepared to win without him.

The game kicked off and we got to a very good start. Everything seemed to be going our way, a feeling that was very familiar to us. As we ended the first quarter up by five points and things going well, I hadn't even noticed I didn't step foot on the court. Yet, I didn't care either because we were winning. The second quarter began and we quickly took a double-digit lead. At this point things looked like they were heading downhill for St. Pat's, but it was still too early to know for sure. I still hadn't got on the court yet, but I was as ready as can be. Anxious as well. A couple of baskets here, a few there, and the next thing you know we are ending the half in a tie game, 21-21.

After I didn't play the entire first half I figured Coach Hurley was so into the game that he just forgot about me. When we went into the locker room at half time he whispered to me, "Shelton be ready the second half." Boy what he didn't know was that I was ready from the tip off. I had never sat an entire half since I played for him ever, shit I never sat an entire quarter since I played for him.

As the second half was under way, I knew I was getting into the game. Third quarter began and the game was close the entire time. In my heart, I knew if I got on the court I would give the team that edge to push forward and never fall back. Coach Hurley told me to be ready so it must have meant I was getting in. Third Quarter ended and still the court was just a pretty sight to see.

When the fourth quarter began, I was becoming more and more anxious. If I didn't think I would be kicked off the team for the next year, I would have just gotten up and subbed my damn self in the game. I wanted to play so bad, I never wanted to play this bad in my life. My eyes were jumping back and forth from the game, to Coach Hurley, then to Coach Gamble. Someone had to notice I still had not touched the court. I just wanted to say Coach, please put me in please, but I knew I couldn't.

As the fourth quarter started to wind down and the crowd noticed things weren't looking too good a loud chant began. "We want Shelton! We want Shelton! We want Shelton!" A spark of hope came through, but still you couldn't tell Coach Hurley what to do. My hopes were very short lived because we ended up losing the game by four. Our dream of a three-peat was over.

We were supposed to win the States and be the Tournament of Champions winners for the third time in a row. I just knew if I had played I would have gave that little edge to win the game. As we entered the locker room I was full of disinterest. I didn't want to hear anything that anyone had to say at all, and my attention was somewhere in the sky or something. I knew how much Coach Hurley didn't like for anyone to yawn and I usually would hide it, but this time I was so frustrated that I could care less. Out came the yawn and Coach Hurley snapped.

"Shelton are you falling asleep while I'm talking? What the fuck is this? I'm sitting here talking and you're in the locker room falling asleep! Get dressed and get the fuck out!"

I began to slowly take my time to get up, I wasn't interested in what he had to say. I was pissed, I wasn't even paying attention at all to what he was saying. All I could do was think to myself. What did I do? Did I do something in school that pissed him off? Was I clowning and he caught me or something? What the hell happened? "Hurry up and get out! MOVE!" I snapped back into it, grabbed my things and left.

Now I can remember being kicked out several times before, but I will never forget being kicked out after the St. Patrick's game. I was upset because I never got on the court, we lost, and our chance at getting our three-peat was now over. I could never figure it out and it left me clueless. Still to this day I can never put it together as to why I didn't play. I had never been so ready to get on the court. I had a burst of energy inside and I just knew if I played we wouldn't have lost. I had a great feeling that night. A feeling I never felt before.

As I was leaving the locker room, I felt I never wanted to step foot in Coach Hurley's gym again. I wasn't sure what I had done, but in my heart, I was sure that I could have helped the team get a win. Knowing that everyone would be outside the locker rooms waiting for us to come out, I quickly walked out with my head down to find my parents and get out of the building. If it were up to me at that point I would have transferred schools immediately. I felt I lost my love for the sport and I desperately needed to find a home where I could recover that love back.

Confused, heartbroken, and just unenthusiastic about playing sports anymore. I came to a point I really didn't know what to do with myself. I had never gotten to a point where I just didn't want to play ball anymore. I was becoming discouraged and I highly felt I needed a change. I thought long and hard about it and I didn't want to leave the guys but when it boiled down to it, I just wasn't into the sport as much as I used to be.

It took a lot for me to bring these feelings to my father but eventually I couldn't hold back anymore. I told him I wanted out and I didn't care where I went. Shit, let me come to Snyder and play there where he coached. He wasn't into the idea of me leaving the school. As we talked about it he looked at me and said, "You were the one that chose St. Anthony High School. I asked you where you wanted to go when you were in eighth-grade and you told me you would be able to do it, so stick it out." I wasn't at all happy with the outcome, but at the end of the day he was right. So, it all boiled down to, "Winners never quit and quitters never win."

2002-2003 Varsity Team
Top: Chris Frazier, Thomas Hall, Obie Nwadike, Sharif High, Terrence Roberts.
Bottom: Derrick Mercer, Barney Anderson, Lamar Alston, Otis Campbell, Marcus Williams, Ahmad Mosby, Shelton Gibbs, Sean McCurdy.

Shelton Gibbs making a move against a defender.

Shelton Gibbs taking a layup against a defender.

Shelton Gibbs shooting a free throw.

Lamar Alston fighting for position to receive a rebound.

Shelton Gibbs taking a layup against Hopkins and Kris Humphries.

Shelton Gibbs Celebrating after scoring an and-one basket vs Lincoln and Sebastian Telfair.

Shelton Gibbs standing in formation waiting for a free throw to be shot.

INTERVIEW IX

When I think about our 2002-2003 team, I think about Sean McCurdy, Coach Gamble and the Lincoln game, the St. Pat's game, and the number four. We lost every game that year by four points.
Still I think that Sean coming to the team threw off our chemistry and brought down the team's morale.
Q: What would you guys say to that?
Beanie: *That year we were still learning how to get used to each other. We were all officially on varsity. You had Terrence, Obie, and Marcus who already had varsity experience. Now me, you, Otis, Thomas, Derrick Mercer, we were all learning. Starting from the summer in the Metro Classic and we lost to St. Pat's that summer. Remember when Coach Gamble told T-Love to go and trap and then Coach Hurley said that was the dumbest play you ever did in your life. Gamble just left Thomas hanging. Ain't even say, Oh I told him to do it. He was in the doghouse that entire year and that happened in the summer time. But yeah, I wouldn't say it was completely because of Sean. We did get side tracked because of his arrival, but at the same time we were all just learning to play with each other.*
Marcus: *That junior year they tried to just fit him in. Things were different. They kept just giving him playing time. They cut Otis's playing time. They kicked Beanie off of the team. It was a lot of things they were trying to figure out due to us and our attitudes. Two of the main players were off the team at certain points. Either kicked off, suspended, or quit. The attitudes at the time was from all the confusion with Sean.*
Otis: *It messed up the chemistry. I stopped coming to practice at one point. I was watching y'all go into practice from my window when you guys would practice at #17 school. It messed the chemistry all up.*

Before the game against Lincoln with Sebastian Telfair, we found out about Coach Hurley's mom being sick and in the hospital.
Q: How did that make you guys feel?
Beanie: *It was shocking to me because then it was like where do we go from here? How is Coach going to be? How are things going to be after this? Is he going to coach us this game? It was just a crazy time. It was pretty much like, where do we go from here now?*
Marcus: *I felt bad for him. We met his mother when we would go to the house. We all knew her. Our prayers were out for him and his family. It was kind of weird to not have him on the sideline coaching us that day. Everybody was concerned, wondering how she was. Concerned for the family.*
Otis: *I felt like damn.* **(Paused)** *Damn. My coach is going through something.*

Q: When we found out Coach Hurley wouldn't be making it to the Lincoln game, did that make you guys nervous?
Beanie: *I wasn't nervous. I was more so trying to figure out what we were going to do to win the game. We are playing against one of the top guards in the country and Coach Gamble is the assistant. He never really head coached the team. Him and Coach Hurley have different techniques. I felt like if Coach was at that game, we would have won that game. He would have figured out a way to slow Sebastian down like we did in the first half. When the second half came, I don't know what changes Coach Gamble made, but it got Sebastian going and he took off. I think if Coach was there, we would have stuck to what we were doing and we would have ended up winning that game.*
Marcus: *I wasn't nervous. I just knew that me being the Captain of the team, I knew I had to keep the guys together. Make sure we stayed focus. That was Coach Gamble's first game coaching us at a very big time playing against Lincoln. I was focus on just trying to make sure everybody stayed together.*
Otis: *It was like Coach Hurley is not going to be here with us, to push us the way we needed to be pushed. Coach Gamble was good, but he's not Coach Hurley. Shit*

changes when Coach Hurley is on that sideline. I felt like he was hurting and we all were hurting.

Q: We wanted to win the Lincoln game so bad to hopefully come home and cheer Coach Hurley up, how did you guys feel when we lost that game?

Beanie: *I felt bad. It was kind of a letdown. We were doing it as kind of like a tribute to Coach Hurley because of his mom passing away. So if we win that game, it was like well here you go Coach. This one was for you. We didn't accomplish that goal. It was a big letdown.*

Marcus: *I felt bad because we lost. We wanted to win it for him and his mom. It was another hit on top of another hit. Our coach loss his mother. Somebody we knew and somebody who blessed us with a great coach.*

Otis: *I felt bad. I felt bad. It was nothing we can do about it. There were certain decisions that were made that game that fucked the whole game up. Taking you out and you were hot, bringing in a cold person, shifted the entire momentum. There were a couple of errors. Sebastian was a great player. We took a couple of hits at one time. It was tough.*

Q: Beanie: When we got to the St. Patrick's game, you had been kicked off the team. What happened then?

Beanie: *I missed a practice and Coach Hurley kicked me off the team. I was supposed to go and talk to him and he told me he didn't want to see my face. Now I'm like, what am I supposed to do? At that point in time, I'm still a teenager. The way he approached the situation threw me over the edge. Everybody was telling me to come back and talk to him, but by then he embarrassed me in front of everybody. It was tough, I battled between going to the next practice and talking to him, but I didn't know where we would go from there. If he lets me back on the team is he going to play me? Am I going to be just sitting on the bench? It was like forget it. I was a teenager, so I really didn't know what was going on. Bad enough, I was making decisions for myself anyway.*

Q: Beanie: How did it make you feel watching that game, knowing you could have made a huge difference?
Beanie: *I was sick! I know if I would have played, not to sound cocky or anything, we would have won. We would have won.*

Q: When we lost to St. Pat's, how did you guys feel?
Marcus: *After we lost to St. Pat's I was hurt. I wanted that three for three. I was already two in. Two Tournament of Champions in. I thought I was about to get three straight. It affected me a lot because I wanted that third straight State Championship. We took it on the chin. After that my motivation, our motivation, me and you guys that came together, was like we not losing next year at all. We all were hungry.*
Otis: *I was pissed off. I was mad as hell. I think I just went and ran in the park. The speech we had after didn't help at all. That game made our mind sets shift. Fuck that we not going out like this next year! We winning! Every game we lost junior year, we came back and won by 20 points or more. I think we probably had four or five games senior year that we won in single digits.*

After we lost to Lincoln, I felt Coach Gamble screwed me over. After we lost to St. Pat's and Coach Hurley didn't play me in the game at all, it kind of put the icing on the cake for me. I began to lose the love for basketball.
Q: Did any of you guys ever feel like the love for basketball was just vanishing?
Beanie: *Yeah, it wasn't fun anymore. It became a full-time job with part-time hours. It wasn't fun anymore. Most of our fun was when we played AAU basketball. When it came to playing for Coach Hurley, it was not fun. It was like, do I really want to do this? It's not fun anymore. It's not exciting. It's too much. I'm not happy with it.*
Marcus: *Nah not me. Basketball was the only thing that kept me going. Basketball was the only thing that kept me going to school. Basketball was the only thing that*

motivated me at the time. If it wasn't for basketball, I wouldn't know where the fuck I would be at. Basketball was everything. I had kids so I was using basketball as a tool. A tool to get out of my environment. To build a future for me and my kids.
Otis: *Yeah, when I moved up to varsity. I wasn't ready mentally for what Coach Hurley was bringing. Coach Hurley yelling like that. Saying I'm not shit. It was more of me having to grow up to take whatever he said. It made you a stronger person and a better player. I feel like I'm a strong person today. I don't let stuff get to me at all. I don't take how people say things, I take what they say.*

THE TEAM 2003-2004: SENIOR YEAR

ALL THE ODDS were against us...

The summer going into our senior year we made a promise to each other and we said no matter what, that we were going to dig our deepest to keep this promise. We promised each other that we weren't going to lose a single game and we would win it all. Marcus came up with this and we all followed. When it came to basketball Marcus was the best leader there could be, he took basketball seriously. This was his ticket out, he needed to take it seriously. He brought us all together to have some words. Sort of like the Mob meeting at a round table.

"Fellas, we finally got here and at this point it's just us! We have been planning this since we came into St. Anthony and we now have something to prove. We have to prove to Coach Hurley that we can win this, we have to prove that we are more than just knuckleheads, and that we can sweep everybody we come face to face with. I don't give a fuck if we play Oak Hill, we have to all bring our A-games and beat whoever we play. If we lose one game, I'm fucking one of y'all up and that's it."

These were the words that came out of his mouth and when he finished he just walked away.

We knew Marcus was serious and he really didn't have to tell us that because we felt the same way, but he had now given us a little more motivation. We were tired of being looked down upon. We should have won everything the year before and quite honestly there were some mistakes made. This year those mistakes weren't going to be made. We had no doubt at all in our minds, no matter what happened we were going to win the Tournament of Champions. We took everything personally.

A distasteful feeling still lingered in my heart from the previous season. This was my senior year in high school, yet I just wanted to get out of St. Anthony and do something else. I wanted to go to acting school to become an actor. I wanted to be like Denzel Washington or Will Smith. I felt the love for basketball was being drained out of me. It was becoming too hard. I didn't want to come home and watch sports. I lived it every single day of my life. Acting interested me, the fact that you could be anyone you wanted to be as an actor caught my attention. So instead of watching sports, I watched movies and television shows. I sat in front of the mirror reenacting movie scenes.

I was confused and I had come too far to just want to up and quit. I went through the motions my senior year with plenty of on and off days. There were times when I was excited about being on the court and other times where I wished the season was over. We spent our last summer together with the Boys & Girls Club and had a good summer with the summer leagues that we played in with our St. Anthony team. We played in an AND1 national tournament and won every game with Otis earning the league's MVP.

This was a start to a great bounce back for our St. Anthony team after losing that big game to St. Pat's last year. We needed every little bit of confidence we could get. Marcus was the only one who was legitimately a two-time State Champion and two-time Tournament of Champion. The rest of us were really moved up our sophomore years and got lucky to be a part of the winning team. Our three-peat was blown and it was now our time to win these championships on our own.

Even after a good summer with the guys, I was still not enthused to get back into the gym for a long season with this St. Anthony program. I wasn't happy at all. I went from almost having a breakout high school career my junior year, to nothing in the blink of an eye. I wasn't playing as well as I knew I could that summer and I was always on edge. Deep down I wanted so badly to get out of that doghouse, but my mental state was constantly bothered.

With Otis having a great summer and winning MVP at the AND1 national tournament, he was in rare form. Otis in my opinion was the best player out of all of us hands down. Even though Marcus was the only one that played varsity ball all four years, I knew what Otis was capable of as a player. We were all good and anyone who felt differently or had anything to say, plain and simply they could kiss our asses. Playing for Coach Hurley was one thing, but when we were outside playing in leagues on our own we were vicious. Otis was vicious.

Under supervision of a great coach and a great program you had to fall in line. If Coach Hurley says to do this or do that, you do it. As a player, you somewhat feel restricted from doing what you know you can do because the coach wants things done his way. You go against Coach Hurley's method, you can play around in the doghouse with the other little puppies. We all knew what we were capable of and what we could do, but Coach Hurley knew how to be successful. Coach Hurley knew how to prepare you for the next level. How to make you become responsible, disciplined, and how to prepare you for life.

As senior year began and that day after Thanksgiving was slowly approaching, Beanie made his way back to the team after sitting on the sidelines watching us lose that St. Patrick's game. It was always rough the first couple of practices because we knew that our first game wouldn't be for damn near a month to follow. This left Coach Hurley with all the room in the world to destroy us for mistakes. See in the season, you don't want to over exhaust the players if they have a game the next day. When you don't have anything for a month, man oh man anything goes. As players knowing this, we would at least try to have the best practices as possible. Yet again with our group, you had no choice but to expect the worst. Even when everything seemed to be going well.

When the first day of practice kicked off, you would expect for it to be golden after having such a good summer. Unfortunately, my grandfather passed away and I wouldn't be at the first few practices. I really didn't like going to funerals at all because death is never really an easy thing. I probably would have been better off going to practice, but the first couple of days in the gym with Coach Hurley were always very demanding. Therefore, I would suck it up and take my bereavement days. As much as I didn't want to see my grandfather lying in his casket, looking as if he was dressed in his Sunday best, I didn't want to hear Coach Hurley's mouth on top of dealing with my grandfather's passing.

Otis couldn't practice because he didn't go to the doctor to get his physical done in a timely fashion. At the last minute, he found out that he had a problem with his heart and had to sit out for some time to make sure everything was okay. I can almost be sure that Otis rather sit out thinking he was about to die, than to be on the court with Coach Hurley being disciplined and scolded on the first few days of practice.

Now normally you would think that a coach would have some sympathy for Otis because after all, he does have a problem with his heart right. Coach Hurley saw right past that one, and we saw past it too. Otis knew damn well he should have taken care of the physical long before the week that practice began. Shit he was probably hoping something was wrong because none of us wanted to participate in that eight-hour coaching clinic Coach Hurley always ran at the beginning of each season.

To add fuel to the flames, I called Beanie to see how the first day of practice went. He told me he stayed in Newark, New Jersey and couldn't get back to Jersey City, so he didn't even go to practice. My thoughts on things were, "Why the hell would you stay in Newark when you know there was practice in the morning and even so, you could have called to say you were going to be late at least." "Easier said than done," Beanie would say and maybe he was 100% right. Either way you looked at it, if you weren't in that gym on time, you were going to get your ass handed to you. A phone call might have showed some responsibility on your end, but Coach Hurley still would have let you have it.

As players, we were so much on edge when it came to Coach Hurley and his basketball team that we didn't think right. We felt that if we were going to be late, we mind as well not show and come up with an excuse as to why we didn't come to practice. After Beanie told me he didn't show for the first day of practice, I was quite sure he would probably be kicked back off the team. Beanie was like a cat with nine lives. Amazingly the next day when I spoke to him, he went to practice and Coach Hurley didn't throw his ass out of the gym. Five lives down, four more to go.

What a way to start the season off. I knew about Otis not being able to practice. I spoke to Beanie about his shenanigans. I guess Marcus and Lamar were doing fine and they would completely fill me in with the exact mood to expect from Coach Hurley. As if anything could be any worse, I get to practice for the eight-hour clinic and there is no Lamar. Me not being at practice, I figured he was excused or something. Nope, Lamar just didn't come to practice for some reason. Supposedly he was upset about something from practice that happened the day before and chose not to come. Here was our crew, at it again with the thing we knew how to do best. Fucking up!

There were two new faces around this year and we of course were standoffish at first. Teacher/Coach Darren Erman and Sports Writer Adrian Wojnarowski. For me these two were part of my inspiration to come to practice every day and at least try to get back into the mode of loving basketball. Coach Erman worked at a law firm making six figures and he quit that career to become a St. Anthony High School teacher and coach. For us, this guy had all the guts in the world for him to do some crazy shit like that. He was the type of person we all wished we could be. A go-getter, a person who just seemed to do what he wanted, a risk taker, someone who lived on the edge and wasn't afraid to take that leap.

Adrian was going to be following the team this year. He was working on a story that covered Coach Hurley and his history with the St. Anthony program, along with covering our season. This was great and even more motivation for us to accomplish our main goals. Going for a perfect season and winning our championships. We figured that if he was going to be following us around, we mind as well give him something to stick around for.

As kids, you are taught not to talk to strangers and that's in any neighborhood, good or bad. At first these guys were strangers to us and we were skeptical about Adrian following us for a story. He was just another snitch to go back and tell Coach Hurley things in our eyes. I mean really, why would anybody want to follow a group of knuckleheads around. Yet after a short while, we began to trust Adrian. He wouldn't run back and tell things, he was really a professional. Sooner or later we didn't even realize he was there half of the time, that's how good he was.

Coach Erman, Adrian, and Sister Alan were like our psych counselors. We could literally talk to any of the three and they would have good advice, or they'd talk to us in that calm manner that we weren't at all used to. The main thing was that they never had to use that statement, "I'm going to tell Coach Hurley." Without them, senior year would have been a disaster for me, maybe for all of us. I would guess that Sister Alan knew exactly how helpful she was, but Adrian and Coach Erman probably had no idea how influential they actually were.

It was time for the season to kick off and our first game was against The Peddie School at Caldwell College. We were all excited about the season starting, yet at the same time very nervous. It was the first game and we had to take the edge off. Shortly after this game we would be heading to California to compete in a tournament in San Diego at Torrey Pines High School. However, we desperately needed to build up our confidence levels before heading out to California.

The game started and pretty much everything went our way this day. We were excited and just having fun. This was the perfect first game for us. We went into the locker room at half time leading the game 52-13. Coach Hurley didn't even scold us or get on our cases about much. This was as rare as seeing Alien life on earth. All I could remember him telling us was not to embarrass the other team. This meant he either liked the coach or had some kind of respect for him. If he didn't like him, our bench probably wouldn't have played and the beating would be one they would always remember. Either way the game ended with a score of 89-36 with Otis having game high of 14 points.

The jitters were out after a 50 plus win over The Peddie School, now it was time to go to California. For kids growing up in the hood, we were doing pretty damn good with traveling and seeing other places. If we hadn't played basketball, we probably would've never seen any of these places at the ages we were. So you could imagine the excitement we all had just to get away from Jersey City into a completely different environment whenever we were granted the chance to.

We took flight to California the day after Christmas. We would have all much rather left on Christmas day because not too long after we landed we had to get prepared for our first game. Talking about tired and just sluggish, yet we knew we still had to do our best if we were going to have that perfect season. As most of us are yawning and just really trying to get ourselves together for the game, Sean is just full of energy. The rest of us are throwing water in our faces and this kid is dribbling the ball back and forth just screaming. All we could do was shake our heads and think what the hell is wrong with him. He always had to do something to stand out and make himself look golden. We all had that 'sit your ass down' look on our faces, but instead of saying anything we continued to shake our heads.

Somehow, we pulled off our first win by over 20 points and after the game all we really wanted to do was get some rest. There would be a lot more time for fun and games the following days. We practiced on the outside courts the next day and we were all happy about that because we figured Coach Hurley wouldn't push us too much being that we were outside. Our next game was against Bishop O'Dowd of Oakland and we were better rested. When we stepped foot in the gym it seemed like there was some sort of tension and we knew everyone was gunning for us. They probably watched us play sluggishly our first game and figured those guys aren't shit. Yet, we all know that pressure bust pipes and we ended up winning that game by over 20 points as well.

We were looking good and at this point ready for fun. We had an early morning practice the next day because Coach Hurley had a full day scheduled for the team. The thing we loved about Coach Hurley was not that he was just a great coach. He was an all-around sportsman. There were times he took us to the football fields and had us playing football against each other. Now we were in California and he had a soccer session scheduled for us. Thinking about things now, none of us probably ever played real soccer in our lives. The closest was probably recreational kickball, where we kicked the ball and ran bases as if we were playing baseball.

We all thought we were pretty athletic and figured how hard could soccer really be? Two guys walked onto the soccer field and they didn't look like much. If anyone should know not to judge a book by its cover, it should have definitely been us. These guys kicked our asses up and down the soccer field. We all quickly realized that soccer wasn't just running up and down a field trying to put the ball in the net. These guys had techniques, foot work out of this world, and hidden strength. One of the guys kicked me in the shin as I tried to do a move with the ball and I felt like he shattered my shinbone. Good thing this didn't count towards our goals of going for that perfect record because they damn sure put on a soccer clinic playing against us.

We enjoyed the session of soccer but one of the most exciting things was that Coach Hurley had tickets to an Oakland Raiders vs San Diego Chargers football game. I think pretty much all of us had never been to a

NFL football game ever and we were overly excited to attend the game. We made sure we freshened up and coincidentally I had a Raiders Jersey back at the hotel. So, I put that on and Ahmad Nivins wore his San Diego Chargers Jersey. We laughed and joked on the way to the game because neither of us were fans of the teams, we just happened to have the jerseys.

I watched football on television and saw how exciting everything looked, but to be in the stadium itself was a different experience. It was completely different than filling up the gym of a high school basketball game. There were people everywhere. Cheering, teasing, and jumping up and down just having a good time. As we were getting to our seats we noticed that the colors in our section were mostly black and gray. We were surrounded by nothing but die-hard Raiders fans.

Ahmad Nivins, standing at around six feet seven inches tall, clearly stood out in this section with his bright colors that he wore as he had on his San Diego Chargers Jersey. I chuckled to myself, man oh man did he make a bad decision of wearing that jersey today. As we figured out exactly where we were sitting, damn near the entire section around us stood up. We were all caught by surprise. A little Hispanic guy probably around five feet three inches tall, looks up to Ahmad and in is tiny little voice with his tattoos on his neck he begins to speak.

"Yo ese, what the fuck is wrong with you? You better take that jersey off and sit on it! This is a Raiders section over here! Take that shit off, put it in the chair, and sit on it!"

As he says that, everyone around us is yelling, "Take the shit off." Ahmad attempts to explain to him that he is not a fan of the Chargers and that the jersey is simply a piece of clothing that he only wore because we were coming to a game that the Chargers would be playing in. The man responds again.

"I don't give a fuck why you wore it! Take it off and sit on it!"

At this point, Ahmad is looking confused because he doesn't know whether this guy is serious or just fucking around. Clearly Ahmad was way bigger than him and probably could have just flung him across the section somewhere, but that most likely wouldn't have been the best idea. Even though we had our entire basketball team and coaches, we were highly outnumbered. Still, Ahmad had that look on his face that expressed he wouldn't be taking shit off and sitting on anything. Suddenly, we heard that very familiar voice. A voice that we recognized over any large crowd no matter where we were or how loud it was.

"AHMAD! TAKE THE JERSEY OFF! PUT IT IN YOUR SEAT AND JUST SIT ON IT! DO IT NOW BEFORE WE ALL GET OUR ASSES KICKED! WE ARE OUTNUMBERED!"

Within the next second, Ahmad took the jersey off and sat on it. I mean if the little guy really wanted him to take the jersey off, all he had to do was tell Coach Hurley because he was the one that could make it happen with the snap of a finger. The fact that there was a crowd surrounding us and we would probably get our asses kicked if Ahmad didn't take off that jersey, wasn't really something we were worried about. Quite honestly, if Coach Hurley wasn't there, the outcome may have been different. We much rather would have gotten our asses kicked for backing up our teammate's decision. Just goes to show how high that respect level for Coach Hurley truly was.

Even with that little confusion at the beginning of the game, we all ended up enjoying ourselves. Of course we teased Ahmad about the situation, but the football game was over and it was back to business. The win over O'Dowd brought Coach Hurley to his 799th win at St. Anthony. One more winning game would give him 800 wins and we planned on doing that right there in California. Our next game was against Flanagan of Pembroke Pines, Florida and we ended up winning by over 20 points. I could remember us winning and Coach Hurley still yelling at someone over a mistake they made as the commentator was congratulating him on 800 wins. What else would be new I thought, but I was happy for Coach Hurley at the same time.

When we won our next game against El Camino of Oceanside, Otis was named the tournament's MVP scoring 19 points. We were so happy for Otis because we knew his struggles and what he was dealing with. Junior year he was literally broken inside and couldn't figure himself out over Sean coming to the school and playing. He had now got himself together and was becoming the player we all knew he could be. I could still see Otis's face and how happy he was, he knew he came a long way. As I stared at him smiling, Otis had that look like he knew it was just the beginning to what he really had to offer to this St. Anthony program.

It was now time to leave California and get back to business at home. We still had a long season ahead of us with so much more to accomplish. Our first home game was coming up against Life Center Academy. I loved playing against Life Center, I always got so anxious to get on the court against them. They seemed to always have a forward and a center each standing at least six feet six inches tall or taller. My junior year I had two dunks against them and one was a put back off the rim over one of the centers. Everyone remembered those dunks and Otis was so hyped for this home game because he said he was getting one of them dunks for certain.

"Shelt, remember you dunked on that tall dude last year! Yoooooo, that shit was crazy, everybody went crazy. Watch, I'm getting me one of them dunks today!"

I responded.

"Chill O, you know you don't have no bounce," a saying we all said that implied you couldn't jump high enough to catch a dunk if you wanted to.

Yet, Otis insisted.

"You crazy, I been dunking all summer, you just watch!"

He was right. He was dunking the ball in the summer and his jumping ability did improve. Now it was just a wait for the perfect opportunity to the basket in order for him to catch that dunk he wanted so badly.

At the beginning of the game Marcus, Beanie, and I carried a banner to center court to present to Coach Hurley for his 800th win in front of our home fans. Otis presented Mrs. Hurley with a bouquet of flowers. After Coach Hurley accepted his banner and said thank you to everyone, it was game time. The game started off well and shortly after tip-off, Otis was granted that opportunity he had been waiting for. As Life Center threw a careless pass, Otis stole the ball and it seemed as if a red carpet to the rim was laid right in front of him.

We all saw the look in Otis's eyes and the conversation in the locker room rushed into my head. Nothing was stopping Otis from this dunk. The second he stole that ball and noticed no one was in front of him, his decision was made. He took off with his eyes lit up like a kid in a candy store. As he dribbled, he was getting his steps down pat so that his dunk is set just the way he wanted it to be. I could hear his voice in my head saying, "Shelt, I'm trying to catch me a Barney dunk!" Which a Barney dunk meant a two-handed cocked behind the head dunk. A dunk that our teammate Barney Anderson would always do when he was underneath the rim.

As Otis took that last dribble and began to take off to the rim, something just didn't go right. Instead of a dunk, Otis took a very awkward looking layup. Afterwards he limped off the court with a painful look on his face. Otis was hurt. Once Coach Hurley noticed everything, Otis was subbed out. We ended the first quarter with a score of 24-6. I was hoping Otis just tweaked his ankle or something small. That way our medical trainer could just tape his ankle up and get him back out, but Otis never returned.

The game ended with an 81-56 win over Life Center even without the presence of Otis. We hoped and prayed that everything would be alright with him. It was very clear that Otis was in pain, yet we really didn't know how bad things were. Otis came too far for an injury to just shatter his dreams. He was at the top of the mountain, everything was going his way. He didn't need to be kicked back down to the bottom with me, it was lonely down there. I hoped nothing but the best for Otis, I wanted him to succeed so much and get over everything.

After Otis's results came back, the doctors said he had a chipped bone on the outside of his foot. Otis was hurt and I was hurt for him. It seemed like we had the worst luck in the world. There was just nothing that could ever be all good with us. Even when it seemed as if nothing in the universe could go wrong, something always went wrong. Now we had to keep it pushing towards an undefeated season without Otis who was at his peak.

I was so happy for Otis. I remembered our eighth-grade teacher telling him he would be throwing chairs against the wall and Coach Hurley wouldn't tolerate his behavior. He had risen above that and again it seemed like it was all stripped from him in a split second. There it was, my buddy was once again down and out. He was lost and confused.

Our next game against Christian Brothers Academy didn't go so smooth without Otis. We ended up winning the game by seven points with some big-time steals towards the end of the game. Beanie had an end of the fourth quarter spark along with Sean which helped us get that seven-point edge over Christian Brothers. It was very clear to us that with Otis things would have been much easier. Already his presence was missed. Not only was Otis out, Lamar was watching the game in the stands. He still hadn't made his way back to the team and it was unclear if Coach Hurley would even allow him back.

To throw a wrench into everything, news got back to us that USA Today had us ranked number two in the nation behind Oak Hill Academy. Coach Hurley made sure to tell us that the ranking didn't mean shit and we still had much more to prove. USA Today could have ranked us number one in the nation and it still wouldn't mean a damn thing. There was only one person's opinion that truly mattered and he had basically just told us we weren't shit. Regardless of who said what or ranked us at what top position, we had to satisfy Coach Hurley. We still had to make him a believer, to hell with what anybody else thought.

We were getting close to playing against Seton Hall Prep who had Brandon Costner, a six foot eight junior as their star player. Miles Beatty, a freshman at St. Anthony, was brought up to play with the team and stir things up. Coach Hurley loved giving you a reason to try to push harder and bring your A-game to the gym. It reminded me of when we were freshman and sophomores and the upperclassmen would tell us how he threatened their playing time with moving us up to play varsity.

Miles was definitely a talented freshman, but his attention span was shorter than the nail on a pinky toe. The kid always seemed to be dazed out or something. Still he had all the energy in the world and he wasn't used to Coach Hurley's system yet, so he played like he normally knew how to play. He wasn't scared to do things and I guess that was a plus for him. From my point of view, certain players had that green light and others needed to play their role. If you had the green light there was more space for mistakes. If you didn't have that green light to go, a mistake would get you yelled at and out of the game.

About a week or two before we were scheduled to play Seton Hall Prep, Lamar was allowed back on the team. Although he practiced the days before leading up to the game, he didn't play. The important thing was that he made his way back with us. Now all he needed to do was stay his ass focus and we had faith that he would. We won the game against Seton Hall Prep 58-52. Now it was time to see how Lamar would play as he made his way back into the rotation.

Everyone kept asking me how I felt about Lamar coming back and if I felt it would interfere with my playing time. I gave them all the simplest answer, no it didn't bother me or I didn't care. I was glad my boy was back on the team. I knew how I could play and I was too stuck in my head about the fact that last year Coach Hurley trusted me to start while Obie was out injured. It seemed like everyone forgot about all of that. Thing is, I wasn't playing the same or with that same intensity, so I see why they would forget. I was broken at that point and still all I wanted to do was be done and move on.

In my heart, I knew I could compete with Marcus, Otis, Beanie, and Lamar at any level. However, to the outsiders looking in, I wasn't as polished of a player as any of them. Which was fine with me and I knew what everyone was thinking, but the reality of it was that I ran out of energy to prove them wrong. I was too weak minded to get myself together and play to my full potential. It hurt inside but I ran out of fight, and I found happiness with being around the friends I grew up with. For me this is how the season would be and I accepted it for myself with no interest in taking that extra step. Looking back at the way things were, I wish I could have been stronger. I was weak with so much anger inside. Yet, the season had to go on.

With Lamar back on the team, it was all up to his work ethic and Coach Hurley's approval of him to get back onto the court. The St. Joseph's of Metuchen game was here and Ahmad Nivins was now eligible to play. We lost Otis and gained two more, man did GOD work in mysterious ways. Leading up to the St. Josephs game everyone was talking about Andrew Bynum. He was predicted to be a McDonalds All-American and word was that he would be going to the NBA. One thing was for sure, Coach Hurley always gave us that confidence that nothing anyone said ever meant shit. This St. Anthony program was all that mattered and we were the ones anyone ever needed to worry about.

We ended the St. Josephs game with a 67-34 win, and Ahmad was happy to be broken in. He was waiting patiently to get his feet wet and it gave him confidence. I still can remember the smile on his face and the look of relief he had. He had progressed so much from when he first stepped foot on the court and I just knew he would get better. He didn't have to worry about the extra shit we had to worry about. Yeah, he definitely lived in our area, but he wasn't really in the streets like we were.

He wasn't a knucklehead or doing knucklehead shit. His future would be a good one as long as he stayed on track.

The Linden game was approaching and bad news came about the night before. Matthew had been shot in his wrist and leg. I knew this came from the drama we were in with the downtown crew and this could have easily been Marcus, Otis, Beanie, Lamar, or myself that had been shot as well. Had we not been on the basketball team getting rest to play against Linden, we may have been out with Matt. The reality of it all was that Matt should have been right with us. He played basketball all this time and just stopped because he felt he wouldn't make it playing for Coach Hurley.

On the court, Matt was a no nonsense, zero tolerance type of guy. Just as if he was in the streets. He couldn't shake that behavior and separate it like we could. I wished he could have because he was just as good as all of us and he should have been a part of our team. Maybe he wouldn't have worked out with Coach Hurley, but he would never find out if he didn't just try. The morning of the game I found out that he would be alright and was relieved of the news. All the guys heard about the incident and I updated them on his progress, so it eased everyone's mind.

It was time for the Linden game and Coach Hurley decided to allow Lamar to suit up for the festivities. It took several weeks, but Lamar stuck it out and pulled through. Unfortunately, Miles had to give up his jersey but he was still only a freshman, he had time. Lamar's comeback wasn't the best. He was unquestionably rusty, in fact the entire game was played like that for everyone. Somehow, we still managed to pull off a 67-51 win.

In the midst of everything with the basketball season and everything going on with different players, Marcus had a secret that haunted him. He was preparing to father his second child. His girlfriend was pregnant with his daughter and he had so much going through his mind. He would talk to us about it, but he worried so much about Coach Hurley finding out. What he did know, was that he would love his children and try to be the best father he could be. The fact that he didn't have his dad around motivated him to try his best. Question was, was he ready to be a father of two at such a young age? Only time would tell.

With so many different things on his mind, it didn't help that he got himself suspended for our next game against Morris Catholic. Marcus skipped out on a midterm exam along with Barney. Coach Hurley always overly expressed the fact that we were student athletes. This meant that being a student always came first. Skipping out on a midterm was unacceptable and they had to pay the price. Good thing it was predicted to be an easy game for us and we still won with a score of 74-32.

Marcus was so worried and at times I could only imagine what was going through his mind. He was always thinking and if he came to a question that stumped him, he wouldn't have a problem expressing his thoughts to his peers at all. Where the problem came in was that we were all kids ourselves, so it was like the blind leading the blind. When he thought about telling Coach Hurley, just like any other issues we had, we convinced him that it wasn't the best idea. Still deep down inside, something told Marcus that Coach Hurley already knew and it was probably true.

Through everything that each one of us dealt with, whether we brought it upon ourselves or not, we knew that basketball had to go on. We moved forward beating Monmouth Regional 71-31, The Hun School of Princeton 62-44, and Raritan 73-55. Next, we would be playing in the gym that brought back memories I dreaded to revisit, the Sovereign Bank Arena. The loss there the previous year against Lincoln tore me up on the inside and still does. At times, I can't remember what occurred in my life the day before or a few hours after it happened. Yet, I still remember the game at Sovereign Bank Arena against Lincoln.

I felt that game in the Sovereign Bank Arena was every single bit of the reason for me to be placed in the doghouse and eventually losing that love for basketball. I strongly felt I was used as a bail out excuse for losing that game. Everything seemed to fall apart for me after that Lincoln game and here we were again playing in the very same gym. Niagara Falls, our opponents, I believe they lost one game for the season and had a few kids on their team that were key players. However, at this point we had tunnel vision. We were still undefeated, any team that wanted to get in the way of that would have to leave with blood dripping from somewhere if they were planning on beating us.

The game ended with a 59-46 victory for us and I was glad it was over. I was sure ready to get out of that gym. The less time I spent in there, the less I would think about that Lincoln game. I was trying so hard to get back into the mode of loving basketball again and the Sovereign Bank Arena was the last place I wanted to be. The moment I walked in there my attitude changed. It seemed like I had a black cloud over my head everywhere I went after leaving that gym the previous year. The win was a plus, yet all I wanted to do was get the fuck out of there.

The next game up was against Our Savior of New American. Games against this team seemed to always be interesting games. This year they had a player that college coaches and NBA scouts showed high interest in. Palacios, Juan Diego Tello Palacios! Palacios was about six feet eight inches tall and 260 pounds. One thing we were confident about was the scouting report on how to contain him in order to get another victory. Coach Gamble always had scouting reports that were out of this world. I mean he broke a team's offense down perfectly. As long as you paid attention to what he was saying, you knew exactly what to expect.

All of the years Marcus played for Coach Hurley, I always remembered him having to defend the best of the best players. For some reason, it wasn't going to be Marcus's job to guard Palacios, but a job for Barney Anderson to uphold. Our defense was always something that carried the torch for us. If our offense wasn't coming together, you better believe our defensive pressure would break a team down. Steals leading to fast break layups, dunks, or whatever. Our defense played a major part in a lot of our wins and it would play a major part in the win against Our Savior.

Otis made his return in the game against Our Savior and of course after not playing in several games he was rusty. Yet, we were all glad to see him back with us. We played against Elizabeth High School and it's always different playing against inner city rough-edged high schools. They come into games not giving two shits about who you are or what you can do. All they know is that they aren't scared and they are coming to play hard-nosed, street/organized basketball. With a sluggish win over Elizabeth, Coach Hurley tore us new assholes. He wasn't satisfied with that win, in fact he screamed at us as if we had lost the game.

The season was coming close to being over and around this time Coach always made sure things stayed tight and everyone had better be focused. It was simply the things he said that would leave your mind boggling at times. Either he really felt you were shit as a player or he said what he said to hopefully motivate you to push harder. There was no one in the world that showed tougher love to their players. No one! Nothing was ever easy, nor could a day in the gym with Coach Hurley be a smooth day. At times, tough love may have been just what we needed. Though there were times a nice gesture or simple words of encouragement would have sufficed, but that wasn't a part of Coach Hurley's methods.

After the Elizabeth game, Coach Hurley went into the whip the team into shape mode. There was no room for mistakes or any bullshit. As mostly all sports players would say, it was "Go hard or go home" time. We won against St. Dominic's of Oyster Bay and beat Neptune after being down for the first time at halftime in a game all season. The Cindy McCurdy/Neptune game, we put on a show and so did she in the stands. Neptune was a big game for us, but a majority of us had the St. Raymond's game on our minds. We were confident that we would beat Neptune, but we all were skeptical about beating St. Raymond. One way or another, we knew we needed to dig deep and get that game under our belts to continue our goal of an undefeated season.

St. Raymond had several players rumored to be going to Division I schools. Yet, here we were ranked second in the nation and not one of us had a clue whether we would be Division I basketball players. Let alone college players at all. For all we knew, we could have ended up either dead or in jail. Still, we needed to beat St. Raymond and after that we felt our goal to an undefeated season was golden.

There was so much talk about us playing against St. Raymond that it made us nervous. Not only the fact that there was so much talk about that game, but Coach Hurley made us seem like we were just okay players compared to the St. Raymond's players. All the players on St. Raymond who had their Division I scholarships already in the workings had to be better than us we thought. Next came the thought of why we even deserved to be second in the nation behind a very talented Oak Hill.

Our minds were very limited to see past all the talk and bullshit. We just started to figure that we were either better than what Coach Hurley made us seem, or we were really shitty players. So for us, beating St. Raymond was everything. It would answer some of our questions and create new questions to be answered. When it was time to play, we got news that one of the Division I prospects got himself suspended. We weren't at all happy about that, now we needed to blow this team out to feel we really should have beat them. If not blow them out, at least beat them by 10 points.

The game started off very well with Barney having a field day leading us to a nearly ten-point cushion to begin with. Our defense always created our best offense and our defense was on point. I don't remember us even getting flustered about chances of game change, because the game was going our way. When everything seemed to be going fine and that ten-point or better lead was there towards the end of the game, there were mistakes made. I can't pinpoint everyone, but I remember Beanie missing free throws and Coach Hurley snapping. The game ended with us winning 54-46, just an eight-point win.

Coach Hurley snapped as if we lost the game. Something we knew oh so well and Beanie had his 'fuck you' face on. I mean after all, it was just a few missed free throws right. We beat St. Ray's, we were happy. Nope, it just wasn't good enough. I didn't quite understand that then, but I understand it now. With that player getting suspended like I stated earlier, we should have blown them out or beat them by more than 10 points. Question was, if he had played would we have even won? Would those missed free throws have been crucial misses? Would those mistakes have been detrimental? Either way, at the time we weren't worried about it, but Coach Hurley sure was.

Two games were left in the regular season and we had no intentions on losing either one. Now it was time to follow the yellow brick road. St. Josephs of Montvale and North Bergen were next up and we felt those would be easy games and confidence builders for the playoffs. Our guts didn't steer us in the wrong direction and we ended up beating both teams. Now this meant the end of the season was just an arm's reach away. Just as bad as we wanted to win the State Championship, Tournament of Champions, and finish everything undefeated, we also wanted to get as far away from Coach Hurley as possible. Coach knew he was tough on us and knew how we felt because he constantly reminded us that those feelings were oh so mutual.

The funny thing about it all was that we all say we felt this way, but I know for myself I wished we could create a St. Anthony College and have Coach Hurley coach us to success on the next level. Even with all the mixed feelings inside about his methods of motivation and his hard-nosed coaching style, I still admired him just as I did when I was a young kid. The fact that it was getting close to the end was starting to kick in. None of us had scholarships in place and I probably didn't deserve one because I played like shit my senior year. With all the hatred and frustration in my heart, I never got out of the bubble I was trapped in. Yet, we still had a goal to chase for the moment.

Hawthorne Christian was our first game of the tournament after we earned a first-round bye. The important thing to some of us didn't even have anything to do with the game. It was the fact that it was Senior Night and we would get a chance to present our parents with flowers at center court. We had come a long way with so much drama, heartache, and pain to get to where we were. To us it was a huge honor just to know we made it as far as Senior Night while playing for Coach Hurley. However, even with feeling honorable the true happiness came from the love at center court, but Otis and Marcus were unsure if they would be able to experience that.

Otis and Marcus's mothers hadn't come to a game all year. They were unsure if either of their mothers would be there at all for the flower presentation. All they talked about that day was just that. The hopes of their mothers being there. The game was just something that had to take place, but that center court moment was special. When both of their mothers were spotted in the gym they were the happiest teenagers in the world and we all were happy for them. I don't think Hawthorne Christian wanted to be on the opposite end of them two feeling untouchable, but they got just that and I think we won by more than 50 points.

St. Mary's of Elizabeth was next in line for our war path towards our championships. We knew St. Mary's would have some scrappy rough-edged players, but we were more concerned about the game to follow. St. Pat's was playing Paterson Catholic and if we beat St. Mary's, which we did, we would play the winner of that game. We all wanted to play St. Pat's because the year before they knocked us out. I especially wanted to play against them. It was still haunting me that I wasn't given the chance to help the team win last year. I felt strongly that if I had played we would have won that game. We were fired up and for myself I felt I had something to prove. If I hadn't given my all in any game all year, this was the game I would do so.

We found out that Paterson Catholic had their way with St. Pat's and our dream of revenge was tossed out the window. For me it wasn't the revenge at all, I needed to redeem myself. I needed to feel like I was wanted. I wanted Coach Hurley to think back to that St. Pat's game last year if he hadn't already done so and say, "Man, maybe Shelton would have made the difference last year." However, this wasn't the case and I was still empty and clueless. I wondered why I hadn't been put in that game. I wondered where the coaching staff's confidence was in me or maybe I had been clowning around or did something wrong for me to not have played. So many different feelings and thoughts left bottled up that I held inside. I figured oh well, Paterson Catholic it is.

This was all for the North Parochial B Sectional Championship and it was a very important game. This was the game to win for us, in our minds once we won this game we would win it all. There weren't any if, ands, or buts about it. Yet nothing could ever just be easy or fall into play. Like my father would say, "If it ain't rough, it ain't right," and of course we had obstacles before us. Sean and Otis were both sick, but no way in the world would either of them tell Coach Hurley. This could have potentially hurt us, but it was a risk we knew we would all take at this point of the year.

Despite the illness in two key players we got an early double-digit lead on Paterson Catholic. It was as if we were possessed. Everything was going well except for the fact that Sean wasn't playing well. With his shortcomings, Lamar stepped up and the crew was back in the spotlight. This was the way we wanted things from the beginning. Even after we accepted Sean, we all felt that he threw a wrench in our system and we also felt he was very selfish sometimes.

Paterson Catholic fought their way back in the second half and made a game out of Sean playing poorly and Marcus in foul trouble. We no longer had a double-digit lead, but Lamar stepped up this day. He was back, and it was a good feeling for all of us. We ended up beating Paterson Catholic 65-54. We were going to win that State Championship. Nothing in the world would stop us now. Our next opponents St. Rose of Belmar had better have some tricks up their sleeves or a miracle that they deserved because no way in the world were we planning on losing this State Championship to them.

We were there, we were finally there. After a long season of hard work and Coach Hurley never letting up on us, we finally made it. From dealing with all the drama in our neighborhoods and within ourselves we were at this State Championship game. No one could tell us that we didn't deserve to be in the position we were in. St. Rose had no idea what we dealt with, and all we knew was that we weren't going to let them strip us of what we felt we deserved. A State Championship banner with an undefeated season.

The side of the backboard and 74-38. Two of the most memorable things about that St. Rose game and State Championship win. Yes, undefeated and State Champions. In the beginning of the game two players managed to shoot the ball and hit the side of the backboard. When this happened, the game was still close. I can still remember the look on Coach Hurley's face. He looked as if he was wondering how they managed to hit the side of the backboard on their shots. From that led to a run that St. Rose wouldn't have a chance of recovering from, 74-38. We were State Champions.

Coach Hurley called Marcus, Otis, Lamar, Beanie, and me to center court to receive the championship trophy. Something that everyone except Marcus only ever got a chance to witness as the previous State Champions received theirs. Now we were added to the group that would have that banner on the wall when Coach Hurley reminded his players that they didn't contribute shit to the previous years of State Champions. We finally did something good, but for us, it wasn't enough. A Tournament of Champions win would seal the deal.

If things went well, we would have two more games left, and everything would be done. Being that we were the top-seeded team, we had a first-round bye and would play against the winners of the Haddonfield vs. Raritan game. We enjoyed our win and gained the chance to walk through Jersey City announced as the St. Anthony State Championship team in the St. Patrick's Day Parade. This was something that made us proud of ourselves, but we still needed to win the Tournament of Champions. It was wonderful being State Champions, but to be State Champions, Tournament of Champions, and have an undefeated year meant the world to us.

The thing that always amazed me with Coach Hurley was that he still pointed out your mistakes even after a win or an accomplishment. He embedded the concept in my mind that even when you think you have done well, there was always room to have done better. With that being said, of course our next practice he wanted us to attempt to hit the side of the backboard in a shooting manner. Yeah, we were State Champions, but how did we manage to look like we didn't belong in the State Championship game by hitting the side of the backboard. Not once, but twice in such an important game. Yet, even when the entire team attempted to hit the side of the backboard no one pulled it off.

With a possibility of only one game left in our senior year, two if we won the first, you would think there wasn't any room for fuck ups or mistakes at this point. We survived to the end just having to finish off the final week, and we were done with the St. Anthony program. It was not only an accomplishment to win the State Championship and Tournament of Champions as an undefeated team, but an accomplishment to win these and have survived through Coach Hurley's madness during our high school basketball years. In the end, we all wanted to look at each other with smiles on our faces and say we did it, we survived. In a perfect world, it would end just like that. Yet, as we know there is no such thing as a perfect world, and we were nowhere near being perfect teenagers.

Lamar pulled off a magic trick. A magic trick that Coach Hurley didn't find to be amusing or intriguing at all. He made himself disappear and was nowhere to be found for practice just days after winning the State Championship. Less than one full week left, and he wasn't at practice. No one had an explanation nor did any of the coaches receive a phone call. Something like this may have seemed insane or the craziest thing ever. There was no reason at this point to not show up. Lamar was just being praised by Coach Hurley for being able to come so far after being allowed back onto the team. How the hell could he have just not shown up? We didn't know but Lamar knew. We all just thought he was bugged out, which is the urban version of the word crazy.

Time was against him, Lamar left his practice stuff home and tried to hurry home to get it after school. By the time he got home, practice was already in session. And like we all figured if it were any of us, we would probably much rather not show up at all then to show up late. Shit if I did show up late, I would have come in, stuck my finger down my throat, and threw up as I was walking through the doors to the gym. Much rather make up a lie than to just show up late. Lamar knew and we all knew it wasn't smart for him to leave his practice stuff home at all, but what was even worse was the fact that he didn't show or bother to call.

Coach Hurley was powerful, and at times it may have seemed like he was too powerful. There was no taking advantage of him and he made us fear being late. Fear making bad decisions. Fear doing certain things on and off the basketball courts. Still, that fear led to bad decisions because what we thought was the best way to handle certain things, often turned out to be the worst way to handle them. With this case, it turned out to be the worst and Lamar was kicked off the team. One fucking week left, with a Tournament of Champions win ahead of us, and Lamar was kicked off the team.

With Lamar being kicked off the team at the very end of the season it bothered all of us, and I think it messed Lamar's head up. We all knew

Coach Hurley was powerful and his word worked wonders. We could only hope that Lamar didn't kill any chances he had to play college ball and move forward in life. It bothered us, but we still had a goal that we needed to accomplish. For me, I was still dragging and just wanting everything to be over. I still had no clue as to what school I was going to or if I would even land a scholarship. We all had issues, and some of us dealt with them in different ways. The only thing that we had was each other and the hunger to accomplish something that we felt everyone doubted we can do.

Raritan earned a rematch against us in what was our first-round game in the Tournament of Champions. The first-round bye led us straight to the final four. We beat Raritan during the season 73-55, so it definitely gave us confidence that we would be able to do it again. The practice the day before that game I will always remember. Coach Hurley wiped my chest with his hand, held it in the air, and let me have it.

"You're not even sweating Shelton!" As he turns to the team.

"This could be his last high school practice and he's barely sweating! How long have we been on the court?"

"HOW LONG?"

Everyone answered, "An hour."

"ONE HOUR!"

"Guess what Shelton, you've done this too many days in high school! This is why we pick up the phone, call schools for you, and college coaches tell us they watched our games and you showed them nothing! That's why nobody is recruiting you!"

He was going off on me, but answered my questions I had for myself. I tuned out of the screaming. Started to think to myself and I knew what he was saying was the truth. I dragged through my entire senior year. Thinking about the Lincoln game against Sebastian Telfair and the St. Patrick's game that he didn't play me in. My mind was stuck in a hole, the love for being in the gym diminished, I was in a slump and I knew it. I snapped back into it, his voice was still echoing through the gym.

"And Lamar Alston isn't with us today! Do you want me to put you in that category Shelton? Do you want to be in that category with the motherfucker who took playing time from you, playing time from Otis? Jerked everybody around! Walked away from it!"

"WE PLAYED SOMEBODY WHO TURNED OUT TO BE A PIECE OF SHIT!"

Not quite sure what the category was that he was talking about, but at that point I just stared with a dumbfounded look on my face. From the sound of his voice, it wasn't a category that I would want to be in. Yet, I dragged through my senior year and didn't care much about anything. When Coach Hurley yelled at me I stared and most times it was in one ear and out of the other. All I needed to do was make it to the end and I would be able to accomplish anything in life.

I left my game jersey on the bus. We were warming up, about to play in the semifinal of the Tournament of Champions and I left my fucking jersey on the bus. With only minutes left in warmups I rushed to the crowd of fans and found my friend Inessa Howell, Ema we called her.

"Ema, please go to the bus and get my jersey. PLEASE! Coach Hurley is going to kill me."

She looked at me, nodded her head okay and took off in a sprint. Coach Hurley had just barked on me yesterday and there was no way in hell I was telling him I forgot my jersey on the damn bus.

"NO WAY IN HELL!"

I was never more nervous in a layup line ever. I wasn't sure if I was sweating from the fact that I was actually working hard in the layup line, or if it was from me being so nervous that Ema wouldn't make it back on time. Three minutes, two minutes, one minute, and my eyes brighten up. Here comes Ema. Sneaking as if she was on a private mission and ensuring

Coach Hurley wasn't looking as the security guard allowed her to give me my jersey. I dodged a bullet and it was game time.

We handed Raritan a loss already and in our minds, we were going to do it again. As much as we tried to ignore the fact that we beat them already and not go into the game as if we had already won, it didn't work. We found ourselves down by double digits for the first time the entire year. Raritan came to play, 15-5 for the end of the first quarter. We knew exactly what was wrong and we had to calm down as a team and take a deep breath.

"I wasn't playing with what I said yo!"

Marcus looked at us as he said those words. Reminding us of the conversation we had in the summer. The conversation from which he stated he was fucking someone up if we lost one game. We came too far and this was not the time to lose at all. Marcus was on a mission and at that very moment he reminded us of what that mission was. Coach Hurley put him on Qa'rraan Calhoun, one of Raritan's best players. Marcus was out for blood and when he said what he said, we knew Calhoun was in for trouble.

The entire team started to get it back together. The defensive pressure and the constant hard work that Coach Hurley demanded paid off. No matter what, the game had to be finished. At halftime, we went from being down 15-5 to up 29-27. The wild animals were let out of their cages. If Raritan even thought they had a chance now, they were sadly mistaken. Once we had our foot on their jugulars there was no letting up. We were out for blood. The second half gave way and the pressure got even more intense. Sean gathered himself together and the animal came out of him too. When Sean was aggressive and wired up, it was a sign that things weren't going to end well for the other team. 56-42 win and heading to the final game of our high school careers.

It was time to put all the negativity, name calling, and bullshit behind us. In our hearts, we knew we could go undefeated, we just knew it. Yet, to make it to the very last game unbeaten still felt surreal. Bloomfield Tech beat St. Augustine to meet us at the Meadowlands for the Tournament of Champions final. Little did Bloomfield Tech know, they would have been better off losing to St. Augustine because this game was personal. The star player Courtney Nelson was a former teammate of ours at the Boys & Girls Club. He left our team and went to play for the Tim Thomas Playaz, and it was something we took personally.

The Tim Thomas Playaz were stacked already, again with J.R. Smith as one of their star players. We were all cool with each other and there were no hard feelings, but for him to leave we took it personally. At the end of the day he wasn't a Jersey City kid and didn't come up with us, but we had every intention on showing him what happens when you turn your back on kids from Jersey City. So unfortunately, his teammates were guilty by association. "Collateral Damage."

Courtney was considered one of best guards in the state. We didn't dislike him at all and was happy for all the attention he was getting, but at times it felt like we didn't get a fair share of anything. Beanie was a great guard. Where was all of his attention? Why is it that all of these players from all of these other teams had scholarships lined up? Yet, us being ranked number two in the nation didn't have shit. Bloomfield Tech got caught in the middle of a ring full of mad men.

Even with all the hearsay about Courtney, we knew we had the answer. Derrick Mercer Jr.! Derrick was one of the best on the ball defenders I've honestly ever seen. He was no taller than five feet eight inches, if that, and could guard you the full length of the court for the entire game. He was a beast on defense, a pure animal. The only one in practice that we stayed away from so that Coach Hurley wouldn't scream on us because Derrick forced us to make a mistake. Courtney Nelson who? Derrick was so confident about his defense that Michael Jordan in his prime couldn't scorch this kid.

A yellowish-orange Lamborghini was pulling away from the Meadowlands. Jason Kidd and the Nets were finishing up in the gym. We passed Richard Jefferson who was full of sweat looking as if he had just got finished doing a triple session work out. Stopping and giving us words of encouragement.

"St. Anthony right? I've heard some good things about you guys. Good luck out therc, and always give it your all."

Maybe in another setting we would have all stopped and asked for autographs, but the words out of his mouth were good enough. We had already envisioned rushing to the center of the court to hold up that trophy and take pictures. We were focused, the only thing that we were nervous and skeptical about was pouring that Gatorade jug over Coach Hurley's head.

The wolves were out, you could see it in all of our eyes. Something that Derrick Mercer Sr. taught us to do when he coached us in our early Boys & Girl Club days. Go up to your opponent at the very beginning of the game. Look him straight in the eye as if you were trying to look into his soul. Once he turned his head away from you, his heart belonged to you for the rest of the game. As far as we were concerned, Bloomfield Tech was soulless, and it was dinner time.

The pressure was on from the very start. Knowing Courtney so well and his style of play, we all could tell that he was nervous. Shit he had better be nervous, the "Tasmanian Devil" was on his ass. Derrick Jr. jumped right into action along with the entire team. You would have thought we had six players on the court playing against five. They were forced to call timeouts, frustrated, and looking confused. The first quarter ended 18-10, at the half it was 33-16. Courtney was the entire offense and without him the team wasn't functioning right.

The third quarter didn't offer anything for Bloomfield Tech either. By that time, we had them on their heels. Like I said our defense was good, but that day our defense was great. At this point the hidden discussion was about who had the heart to pour that Gatorade jug over Coach Hurley's head. With nearly a 20-point lead towards the end of the fourth quarter, we all felt like we had accomplished the biggest thing we would ever accomplish in our lives. Pleasing a man that we felt could never be pleased. 67-55, the game was over, we had gone unbeaten. 33-0.

We rushed to that center court. Jumping, screaming, smiling, and laughing. This was much more to us than just an undefeated season. Much more to us than basketball itself. It was hard where we came from, and everywhere we turned negativity had its hand on us. The drugs & alcohol, the violence, the filth all over our streets, the absence of guardians, and the proper guidance. It all meant nothing to us now. We now knew that if we worked hard enough, we could accomplish the unthinkable. Just hold your head high, believe in yourself, and fight against all the odds.

The locker room was a mad house. Soda and water being tossed all over the place. We still were debating as to who the hell was going to give Coach Hurley his Gatorade bath. In the midst of the celebrating Coach Hurley walks into the locker room, and just like always we all looked at him and there was nothing but silence. Coach spoke, we listened, and no Gatorade jug was being lifted over this man's head at all. It was then we truly realized that no matter what, Coach Hurley would always be respected.

In the press conference room, Marcus, Otis, Beanie, and I were all being interviewed. Coach Hurley asks, "Did any of you think we would go undefeated?" We knew the exact answer he wanted to hear with the way he asked the question, so we all answered no. Truth of the matter was, we all knew we would go undefeated. That was our number one goal, next to trying to gain Coach Hurley's heart back.

After we left the conference room, we all slapped each other's hands and hugged. Almost simultaneously we all said, "Damn, wish Lamar was here," but somehow in our hearts we knew that he was a part of this accomplishment. As we made our way back to the locker room, we were never happier than now to be called St. Anthony Friars. Together as teammates, for one last time, we recited our Catholic School prayer we would say before and after each game.

"Hail Mary, full of Grace, The Lord is with thee.
Blessed are thou among women,
And blessed is the fruit of thy womb, Jesus.
Holy Mary, mother of GOD, Pray for us sinners,
Now, and at the hour of our death.
Amen!
Lady of Victory, Pray for us!
St. Anthony, Pray for us!
ONE! TWO! THREE!
HARD WORK!"

2003-2004 Varsity Team
Top: Qaysir Woods, Justin Lewis, Ahmad Nivins, Ralph Fernandez, Robert Bullock, Eric Centeno, Barney Anderson, Linoll Mercedes. Bottom: Ahmad Mosby, Derrick Mercer, Shelton Gibbs, Sean McCurdy, Otis Campbell, Marcus Williams.

Coach Hurley receiving his 800th win plaque. 2003-2004 season.

Marcus Williams making a move against a defender.

Ahmad Mosby taking a layup.

Marcus, Otis, Shelton, Ahmad, and Lamar enjoying dinner after 2004 State Championship win.

Marcus Williams, Shelton Gibbs, Coach Bob Hurley,
Ahmad Mosby, and Otis Campbell receiving Tournament of
Champions trophy after Bloomfield Tech game. 2003-2004 season.

INTERVIEW X

Marcus, the summer before our senior year, you gave us a pep talk. You basically told us that we had better not lose a game this season at St. Anthony and if we did you were going to kick one of our asses.
Q: What were your overall intentions when you made that statement?
Marcus: *To make everybody hungry. I took the losses from junior year, me not getting the third State Championship, and I just knew that somebody had to stay on top of us to keep us hungry. AAU was AAU for us, but playing for St. Anthony High School meant a lot to us. Let's not lose the hunger. The hunger should have stayed in all of us after the losses junior year. We came in fifth place with AAU. We not coming in nothing but first with St. Anthony.*

Truthfully, I felt that we were all good enough to play anywhere besides St. Anthony and average double digits. I felt like sometimes we were held back from doing things we were capable of doing. Coach Hurley made us fall in line and play the role he wanted us to play.
Q: What would you guys say to that?
Beanie: *Yeah, of course. Prime example, there are guys in the NBA right now that we played against in AAU basketball and when we had free will we made them look bad. Real bad! They are making millions of dollars right now and we made them look bad. I guarantee you, until this day, they all remember us. They can front like they don't remember us, but as soon as you say Boys Club, they'll be like oh shit. "Nah, I don't remember." Ohhh you remember! Yeah, we were held back.*
Marcus: *Playing for any other school we would have did what we wanted to do. Playing for Coach Hurley, you got to play within a system. The system held us back because you have to run your plays to the tee. He only calling plays for certain people anyway. If you do score or you are getting points, you getting that off of rebounds, loose balls, or steals. If plays are not called for you or if his system is not designed for you, you're not going to be noticeable. If we would have went to any other school, then coaches would have been loving us. You would have all the freedom in*

the world. Playing for St. Anthony you have to play within Coach Hurley's system and that system holds a lot of people back.

Otis: *With St. Anthony, there is structure. This is the game plan, you stick to it, you're going to win. Sometimes that free for all stuff, that shit backfires. You might not be on that night. They are doubling you, you don't got this shot. Yeah, he held us back from playing like we would play outside in the parks, but I also felt like we needed that structure. With the structure mixed with some freedom, it was like a bomb waiting to explode. When it did we never lost. I wouldn't say he held us back, I would say it was needed for the type of players we were.*

I feel like Sister Alan, Coach Erman, and Adrian were like our psych counselors and motivated us to keep pushing our senior year.

Q: What are your thoughts on that?

Beanie: *I would say yes to Coach Erman and Sister Alan. I don't know about Adrian. I think Adrian was just trying to absorb everything in for his book. He was listening to us, but it was for a reason. But Sister Alan was like that from day one. She would get on you in school. Then she'd be like, come on guys, you know you need to do this, you need to focus. You need to do this, you need to do that. She was one person you could talk to, but don't tick her off.*

Marcus: *They did. Sister Alan was a great woman. She always talked to me in a positive way. Telling me I'm doing good and to keep up the good work. Sister Alan had been around Coach Hurley for years. She knew all of the other kids that went through him. She talked positive to us just to motivate us. Telling us to keep doing good. Coach Erman was there to learn, but he also knew some of the guys couldn't handle that pressure. So he gave us good conversation and positive talks as well.*

Otis: *Yeah, they were more like extended family. All the things Adrian saw and we told him. He could have said a lot more. He kept his word though. He said,* ***"I'm not going to put anything in the book to make you guys look crazy. I just want you to give me the real story."*** *He would come to my house and sit with me. Sister Alan used to say,* ***"I've been here for a long time. Believe me when I say he's like this with every kid that comes***

through St. Anthony. Don't feel bad." *I brought her my bags with all of my stuff one day and said, I quit Sister! I don't think I'm going to be here next year!* **(Laughing)** *She looked at me like, oh no. Let me talk to you for a minute. She took me in the office and we sat down and talked. She made me feel like I wasn't the only one who ever felt the way I felt. He's done this to everybody. Take your bags, go to practice, and just deal with it. Things will get better.*

Q: How did you guys feel when you found out Sister Alan was sick?
Beanie: *I was hurt by it. Not for nothing, Sister Alan was like a mother to us at school. She became family.*
Marcus: *Sister Alan was my roll-dog. She kept me out of a lot of trouble. She was there for me all my years at St. Anthony. That right there hurt. Knowing that she was going through what she was going through.*
Otis: *I was hurt. It messed me up. Sister Alan was the heart and soul of St. Anthony. The heart and soul. If it wasn't for Sister Alan, we all probably would have been kicked out of school.*

Q: When we found out Adrian would be following us, I think we were all surprised and excited, would you guys agree?
Beanie: *I was souped! I was souped up! Like, Word! Word, we are going to be in a book. We going to be what! Oh, yeah! I'm down with this. We definitely going to always be remembered. Outside of winning. We can walk into Barnes & Noble, hold up the book and say, Yeah. That's me!*
Marcus: *I was excited to have somebody following us around our senior year. I thought it was dope. I was thinking big. I'm thinking book, movie. Every game we are winning and he following us. Undefeated season. Camera crews coming. It was very exciting.*
Otis: *I was happy as hell. We never had exposure like that. As far as being in a book. I was happy as hell. I was like, when is it coming out. That is something that a lot of players don't get. We got some shit that's in the history books right there. Especially as far as St. Anthony. Read that right there. Read that.*

Otis, shortly after we got back from California, we played against Life Center. You asked me before the game if I remembered catching the two dunks against them the year before. You were so anxious and said you were going to catch one of them dunks.

Q: What happened when you got that opportunity? What went wrong?

Otis: *I planted wrong. I had a stress fracture. A stress fracture starts like a little crack in your bone and over time it gets longer and longer. Then it breaks. I had a stress fracture already and I didn't know. You don't feel it until it's too late. Once I planted my foot, I knew. I felt it. When I planted to go up, I felt a snap. That's why I laid the ball in the way I did.*

Q: Otis, when you got hurt, what was on your mind?

Otis: *I was fucked up. In my head, I was hurt because I felt like I need this year. Coming off of a great summer. I need this year. I was number four in the State. Top shooting guard in New Jersey. This was the year I was waiting for.*

Q: Otis, when you came back after your foot injury, how did you feel?

Otis: *I was just happy to be back a part of the team. I still felt out of the loop a little bit. There wasn't enough time for me to get back into everything. I was coming off of the bench and I wasn't at the top of my game anymore. When I came back, the level I was on was nowhere near the level I was at. I wasn't getting interviewed or sitting in on press conferences. I didn't let it bother me because I was just happy we were winning. I knew I had to get my foot back right. I was just happy we were winning.*

I think it was the night before our game against Linden and Matt got shot. I always felt that if we weren't playing ball and in the streets with Matt, that could have easily been one of us.

Q: What are your thoughts on that statement?

Beanie: *That could have been one of us most definitely. It was all over the bullshit we were into. That could have been one of us. Nine times out of ten, whatever was*

going down with Matt, we would have been involved. It probably would have escalated into something bigger with all of us being there. Who knows?
Marcus: *Matt should have been with us. He didn't want to even play basketball anymore. I don't think he wanted to deal with Coach Hurley. If we weren't playing basketball, we all would have been right there.*
Otis: *That was a strong possibility. We were all together a lot. Matt didn't want to play ball anyway. He played because we were all always together. I knew him and Hurley were not going to click. I guess he knew it too, but he didn't want to leave the school because we were there.*

We were ranked second in the Nation behind the very talented Oak Hill, and playing against teams that were ranked lower than us. Yet, we had no scholarships lined up and it seemed like everyone else did. From Oak Hill to the lower ranked teams.
Q: How did that make you guys feel?
Beanie: *It didn't make sense. It didn't make sense to me. I get it, maybe a few of us didn't have the grades, but some of us did have the grades. I don't understand why there were no scholarship offers. I didn't get it. We are undefeated, number two in the Nation.* **(Paused)** *Coaches should have been knocking at the door. Like I said, dudes we played against had scholarships, got offers to all types of schools. It's not like they were better than us. Some were worse, and some were equal. Why was nobody knocking on my door?*
Marcus: *I felt fucked up. We are putting in all of this work and we are not being noticed. Knowing that we are coming from St. Anthony High School, you should want to have one of us on your roster. Maybe it had to do with grades for some of us. I know for me it was my grades. Overall it was frustrating, it was annoying.*
Otis: *It made me ask myself, what are we doing wrong? We are winning, putting up big numbers, and playing for St. Anthony. What are we doing wrong? We got letters, but they were the computer-generated letters. I felt like, Damn. What is going on here?*

Marcus and Otis, I remember senior night and you guys being nervous that your mothers wouldn't make it.
Q: How did you guys feel when you saw your mothers in that gym?
Marcus: *It meant a lot to me. I always felt like I wanted what you guys had. You guys that had your parents coming to the games. To me it meant a lot because my mother never came to nothing. I wanted her to be at every game, but unfortunately, she was raising three kids by herself. She couldn't come to the games. It meant a lot for me to see her at the game for my senior night.*
Otis: *I was happy. When I called her, she said she wasn't leaving work to come to the game. I knew she had to work, so I couldn't get upset. When I saw her walking across that court, I was like damn. My mother came to the game. I used to just show her my tapes. I was happy. Hell yeah I was happy.*

Q: Beanie and Otis, how important was it for us to win that State Championship and not worry about hearing, "You guys didn't contribute shit to the previous years of State Champions?"
Beanie: *After we won the State Championship, I felt like, AHHH HAAA! I thought we were going to lose. But I realized my high school career was over. It's not like coming out of grammar school and playing AAU together. After high school, we had to branch off and do what we had to do. It was very important. Very important. All season Coach Hurley kept saying he didn't think we were going to win. He even said it when we won.*
Otis: *We in the history books. We have our own legacy now. We have something to talk about when we are around other players. Well we won the states. Oh yeah, we won too. By 30 points and the Tournament of Champions.*

Q: How did you guys feel when we lost Lamar with only two games left to win the Tournament of Champions?
Beanie: *To be honest, at that point in time I wasn't focus on L. I wanted to win still. It was like bro, at this time in the season, you can't be doing this. We are about to win. What are you doing? Stay focus!*

Marcus: *Losing him meant a lot to me because I was closer to Lamar than everybody. He had his ways. He had a lot of things going on with him as well. He had a kid at a young age. He got his step pops always on top of him. His step pops wanted the best for him, but he wanted to go his own way. For Coach Hurley to kick him off the team or he quit, it was bothering me because I was close to him.*

Otis: *He was the reason we got there. He played good in the State Championship game. Maybe there was something going on. Something that we didn't know at the time. It had to be. You're the reason we won the States and off the team right after that. This is our last year.*

Beanie, from my point of view you were better than so many of the guards that got so much attention.

Q: Did that bother you that some of them was so highly talked about and had Division I scholarships lined up when you had nothing?

Beanie: *Yeah, it bothered me. I knew all year around, even in the AAU circuit, that they didn't want no parts of me. No parts! It was, oh boy, I got to play Beanie today. He's going to get on my nerves. He's going to hound me all day. He might make me look bad in front of my parents. Then you see, he's going here, he's going there, and what about Beanie. Where are you going? It was frustrating. But it was Coach Hurley's system. Those kids had free will to do what they wanted. You put us in their shoes, we would probably look perfect. Playing for Coach it was like we were just regular players. Coach Hurley is the reason why they are winning.*

Q: Our team was phenomenal on defense, but how good of a defender was Derrick Mercer Jr.?

Beanie: *Boo used to strap up. I don't care what you say. He used to strap up. He was short so he was already low to the floor. He used to squat even more. Try that low crossover if you want. It's going to be sitting right in his hand. He used to lock people up something serious.*

Marcus: *To me that's the best defensive player I ever played with. Hands down! One on one, couldn't nobody get past him. His pops got him like that. He was the smallest player. He was the best one on one defender I ever played with.*

Otis: *He was the best point guard I ever saw on defense. The best I've ever seen on defense. The best I ever played with. You say Boo, don't let him score, don't let him get the ball up the court. He would take that shit and get in the zone.*

I remember having several discussions that if we won, we were going to dump that Gatorade jug on Coach Hurley's head.

Q: Why were we so scared to do it?

Beanie: *That went out the window. The first thing we thought about was what's going to happen if we do that. We still don't even have schools to go to. I throw this jug on him, I'm really not going nowhere. I might have to get a job.* **(Laughing)**

Marcus: *We didn't want no parts of Coach Hurley. I guess we thought we were going to get yelled at. Even though we didn't have to play for him no more. I don't know why we didn't do it.* **(Laughing)**

Otis: *I was waiting for one of y'all to do it. I wasn't going to be over there. You crazy as hell!* **(Laughing)** *I never saw that shit happen to him. I never saw nobody dumping nothing on his head. Hell no! Hell no! I would have done it to Coach Erman.* **(Laughing)**

I felt like when we won it all and went undefeated, it was the only time we made Coach Hurley Happy.

Q: What would you guys say to that?

Beanie: *I guess it was a weight off of his shoulders. He probably was happy that he was done with us.* **(Laughing)** *I don't even think it was about winning.* **(Laughing)** *He probably was like, they won. Good! I don't have to deal with these knuckleheads no more.* **(Laughing)** *We stressed him out.*

Marcus: *I don't know. I don't remember seeing him happy. I don't know. He didn't show much emotion. Hopefully knowing we were graduating and leaving made him happy.* ***(Laughing)***
Otis: *He was happy. He smiled. He never really showed emotion and I saw him smile.*

Q: When we were in the interview room and Coach Hurley asked us did we know we would go undefeated, why did we all say no?
Beanie: *We weren't arrogant like that. We made it seem like it wasn't that, but in our heads, we knew we were going to win.*
Marcus: *We thought that was the right thing to say to him. We knew amongst each other. He wasn't in the locker room after we lost and we said we are going undefeated here on out. For us, we had a goal. When he asked us, we thought that was the right thing to say. That's why we gave that answer.*
Otis: *We didn't want to come off arrogant or cocky. I could remember us saying that we aren't losing no more. Way before the season even started. Way before the summer and it just played out. We said no because that was the right thing to say.*

I must say it was an honor playing side by side with you guys for all those years we played. I am very appreciative to have been friends, forget friends, brothers with you guys for all of these years. I would not trade in any of our relationships for the world and will always love you guys.
Q: My final question to you is, how did you guys feel when you found out that St. Anthony would really be closing the doors this time. I mean I always figured that if Coach Hurley still had air to breathe, those doors would never close. How did this news make you guys feel?
Beanie: *I felt like, really! How? How would the city alone let that happen? Let's be honest, St. Anthony kept the city on track. Not for nothing, that's what*

Jersey City is known for. Remember they had the sign when you are coming over the bridge on 1&9. "Welcome to the Home of the St. Anthony Friars." St. Anthony put Jersey City on the map. Everybody liked to see us play. You had drug dealers coming to the games and at that moment it kept the streets safe. Also, it changed a lot of lives. Like the inner-city kids. If you look at the St. Anthony team now and for the past few years. Guess what! You got kids coming from different towns to come play. When we were playing, all the kids were from the local area. A lot of kids were growing up saying I want to play for St. Anthony. St. Anthony closes, the city is going to go to the dumps. That's how I see it. I don't see how the city is allowing that. Forget the city, the State. Coach Hurley put New Jersey on the map. I don't care about no other high school or University. When you think of high school basketball, you think of St. Anthony, Bob Hurley, and Jersey City. Period!

Marcus: *There's a lot of memories with St. Anthony. Not even basketball memories. In school memories. Hearing that it's closing is touching. You think about all the things we went through and did. I had fun my four years there. All I could do now is look back and say I had fun there.*

Otis: *Hearing that messed me up. That school was a savior to my ass. I never thought that school would close. It's going to be an emotional moment. If I had the money, the school wouldn't be closing.*

Interviews were conducted after the completion of the book. None of the interviewees were ever all in a room at the same time. None of the interviewees discussed the interview questions prior to the interviews. None of the interviewees were granted the opportunity to read the book prior to the interviews.

June 2017, Shelton Gibbs at St. Anthony High School's final gathering before the school closes along with the 2004 Tournament of Champions trophy.

WHERE ARE WE NOW?

After High School, we all remained very close friends. Milly was arrested shortly after having a daughter and sentenced to about 20 years in prison. We all have spoken to him occasionally and we are waiting for the day he finally comes home.

Matt encountered two more near death experiences after high school. He was shot multiple times in his abdominal area and in his legs. Luckily, he survived both shootings. He was arrested and served three years in prison. He now has a son and he maintains employment.

Lamar moved to Alabama after high school. He bounced back and forth from Alabama to New Jersey for five years until he finally decided to move back to New Jersey. He has seven children and currently working towards owning his own business.

Marcus went on to play basketball at Globe Institute of Technology in New York City for two years. He later attended and played basketball at St. Francis College in Brooklyn, New York. He has three children and is currently a Lead Dock Worker at a warehouse in Jersey City.

Otis played basketball at Hutchinson Community College in Kansas for two years. Along with Marcus, he also attended and played basketball at St. Francis College. He has two sons and is currently a Dock Worker at the same warehouse Marcus works at.

Beanie attended Ramapo College of New Jersey. He played basketball there for three years and left school after his junior year. He coached high school basketball for a few years and is currently a Security Guard.

I attended Dominican College of Blauvelt located in Orangeburg, New York. I played basketball there for four years and had my son Shelton III in 2010 with my college sweetheart. We jumped the broom in April of 2016. I am currently working as a Firefighter in New Jersey for the Hillside Fire Department.

A LETTER TO COACH HURLEY

Coach Hurley,

In so many ways I am grateful to have played basketball for you and granted the opportunity to learn from the greatest. As a kid, I remember having my first pair of Iverson sneakers because you had an extra pair left over from the team sneakers. You have been a wonderful friend and role model to my family for several years. I must be completely honest, I didn't understand you as a player on your team. I didn't understand your methods, your passion, and aggression. I was too immature for your motivational methods at the time. Unsure as to whether you even cared about Marcus, Otis, Lamar, Beanie, and me. As I matured, I realized what everything meant. I realized that all you were trying to do was push us harder to give it our best. One thing I always liked about you, was that no matter if we were winning by 30, you still coached. We could blow a team out of the gym and when the game was over, you still pointed out the numerous mistakes. Demanding that they be fixed. You showed us that a good performance always had the opportunity to be a great performance. That our best could always be better. There were times I wished you had let up on us, but you never did. You were stern and demanded so much. And oh yeah, we were definitely a crew of knuckleheads, I cannot disagree with you on that at all. Which is why I understand that you couldn't let up on us. As much as I hated all that pressure,

I loved it all the same. It amazed me that you had college coaching opportunities, NBA coaching opportunities, yet stayed at St. Anthony. It showed so much dedication, loyalty, and love to the city of Jersey City. To St. Anthony and the young men that came through your program. To the future star athletes that dreamt about learning from Coach Hurley. Even after St. Anthony, your players carry over the discipline we learned from you into our everyday lives. Be early, be presentable, look at someone when they are talking to you, be responsible, strive for the best, for perfection. Plenty of Jersey City kids didn't have father figures or anyone to show them the way. They didn't have anyone to discipline them, anyone to be there and hold them accountable for their actions. All they knew was that they wanted to play ball. Who would expect to come to St. Anthony and gain not only the knowledge of the sport, but gain that father figure that some needed so bad. To be introduced into a family that actually cared and wanted to see them progress. The Friar Family.

In 2012, I went on an interview for the Hillside Fire Department. During the interview one of the Deputy Chiefs asked me about the Championship ring I had on and stated that they saw on my resume that I attended St. Anthony High School. I responded, "Yes I did." They then asked why I didn't list you as a reference, because they would have loved to call and talk to you. I told them that being a player of yours I learned to have honor, work hard, be disciplined, and take responsibility for my own actions. I stated that though I would have loved to put your name on my resume, I rather not because I take pride in what I learned from you. I finished off with, "But I can call him if you want me to, I do have his number in my phone." I was very intrigued that even after eight years, you still played a role in my life. I laugh about it now, but what I didn't tell the Deputy was that you would probably tell him I was a knucklehead and it would hurt my chances of becoming a Firefighter. I am very fortunate to have met the group of guys I work with. To be a part of the Fireman's Mutual Benevolent Association and Hillside Fire Department is an honor. The discipline and hard work that you demanded really did pay off. There was nothing that has been put in front of me that I felt I couldn't handle. Playing for you and learning from you has made things easy for me and even when it's not easy, I wouldn't back down from the challenge.

Coach Hurley, I thank you for all that you have done for me. I thank you for all the Jersey City kids that you have guided into the right path and granted them with opportunities that they most likely would have never had. It was a pleasure and an honor to play basketball for you. Learning from you was not only beneficial to the sport of basketball, but beneficial to my everyday life. You demanded discipline and hard work, and without that I would probably not be where I am today.

Thank You Coach, for everything.

Shelton T. Gibbs

ACKNOWLEDGMENTS

THROUGHOUT MY YEARS, I have met some wonderful people. I have played basketball with so many different athletes and have had some wonderful experiences. Still, nothing can compare to the experience I had playing at St. Anthony. Without Coach Hurley, Sister Alan, the coaching staff, trainers, teachers, parents, students, and players, this extraordinary Friar Family would not exist. It saddened me to hear the news that the little school downtown on eighth street was shutting its doors. St. Anthony was not just a school for basketball as some may think. This school saved the lives of several Jersey City kids that I myself grew up with. When you walked in the doors you felt safe. You felt like you were away from anything that you saw or heard when you got back home at night. For some, St. Anthony was not an option, but a must. A must because some of the students wouldn't last in some of the public schools' close to their homes. Without the Friar Family, I would not have been able to express my feelings through this book. I thank Marcus, Otis, Lamar, Milly, Matt, and Beanie for participating with me in telling our story. I thank Coach Hurley for instilling the discipline and hard work in us. For being so demanding and pushing us to succeed. I thank the Hurley family for allowing a son, a brother, an uncle, a cousin, a husband, a father, a grandfather, into the lives of so many youths in Jersey City. Thanks to my family for always supporting me and having my back no matter what I do. Shelton Sr., Elyse, Shellyse, and Shyquan Gibbs. My brother and I will always be able to debate which undefeated team was the best, the 2004 team or the

2016 team. I could certainly say that the 2016 team has the better rings, but uncertain about anything else. A special appreciation to my wife, Ashley Gibbs, and my son, Shelton Gibbs III. Thank you guys so much for supporting me and sacrificing some family time, which granted me the opportunity to write this book. I love you both. Thank you, Ashley, for staying up for countless hours to listen to my story and encouraging me to continue on. To my long-lost friend from elementary school, I have never stopped thinking about you. Wondering if you are safe and how you made out in life. Wondering if you are even alive. I kept my promise and never told, but today I am unsure if that was the best idea. A special thank you to Gary Greenburg and the Boys Club family. Frank Burno, Joe Whalen. Thank you guys for always believing in us. Having faith in us. You granted us with opportunities that plenty of kids from Jersey City never got the chance to experience. Your Boys Club kids love you guys. Thank you to Adrian Wojnarowski and Coach Darren Erman for inspiring us to become great. Showing us that a dream doesn't stop at just a dream. That we can make that dream come true. To the entire Hillside Fire Department. I thank you so much for granting me the opportunity to become a part of the Fire Service family. For making me feel great and allowing me to be a part of a family that's beyond this world. For supporting me through my process of writing this book. Thank you to Cheyenne Bostock for providing me with the steps to publish my book. Cheyenne is a Life & Relationship Expert and a former St. Anthony teammate of mine. Please visit his website askcheyb.com. Last but not least, I would like to thank my sister again, Shellyse Gibbs, my editor, Sydney Morgan, the fiverr community, and createspace.com for bringing my book to life.

To my Grandparents,
Adele Jordan and William Jordan.
Mary Gibbs and William Gibbs Sr.
I love you guys dearly.

CPSIA information can be obtained
at www.ICGtesting.com
Printed in the USA
BVHW03s1931160818
524747BV00001B/101/P